Prayers to the Holy Angels

"The Human Soul" by Luis Ricardo Falero (1894).
Courtesy Wikimedia Commons.

Prayers to the Holy Angels

**ADAPTED & COMPILED FROM
APPROVED SOURCES**

BooksByNoël.com

"St. Gabriel the Archangel" by Hubert van Eyck (circa 1426).
Courtesy Wikimedia Commons.

Prayers to the Holy Angels

ISBN-13: 978-0-9893310-7-4

Interior design & typesetting: Fletcher & Co. Publishers
Photos: Marie Noël
Cover image: "The Angel" (19th century) by Carl Timoleon von Neff, courtesy Wikimedia Commons.

Fletcher & Co. Publishers, www.fletcherpublishers.com
First Edition

CONTENTS

Chapter 4: All Holy Angels   70

Chapter 5:   All Archangels   109

Chapter 6: St. Michael the Archangel   114

Introduction

This collection of Catholic *"Prayers to the Holy Angels"* focuses on seeking the intercession of the angels. It contains prayers to our Guardian Angels, the Nine Choirs of Angels, the Archangels (St. Michael, St. Gabriel and St. Raphael) and more. Included also are prayers which an angel taught to the children at Fatima. Also featured are prayers to God and the Blessed Virgin Mary, Queen of the Angels, which invoke the holy angels.

The existence of angels is a truth of the Catholic faith. Angels are spiritual beings without bodies. "As purely spiritual creatures, angels have intelligence and will," notes the *Catechism.* "They are personal and immortal creatures, surpassing in perfection all visible creatures, as the splendor of their glory bears witness." Angels are inferior to God, but superior to mankind in knowledge and strength.

The holy angels are frequently mentioned in Sacred Scripture. The Archangels Michael, Gabriel, and Raphael are mentioned by name. We can pray to the angels to intercede for us and to place our requests before the throne of God.

Devotion to the Nine Choirs of Angels is an ancient practice in the Roman Catholic tradition. The Nine Choirs consist of the Seraphim, Cherubim, Thrones, Dominations, Virtues, Powers, Principalities, Archangels, and Angels. Each type of angel has a special office (mission) and belongs in one of three hierarchies:

- 1st hierarchy—the Seraphim (the ardor of love), Cherubim (fullness of knowledge and science) and Thrones (divine peace).
- 2nd hierarchy—the Dominations (dispense God's orders from on high), Virtues (strength to enable people to carry out these orders), and Powers (appointed to fight against evil spirits and defeat their plans.) They are more focused on human affairs.
- 3rd hierarchy—the Principalities (guard nations and govern souls), Archangels (tasked with important missions and protection over people and the Church), and Angels (Guardian angels and messengers to people).

"Angels in Altarpiece" by Simon Vouet (1625). Courtesy Wikimedia Commons.

The Catholic faith holds a special place for the angels in our devotions. According to our tradition, each day of the week and month are consecrated to a particular devotion. For instance, Tuesdays are dedicated to the holy angels, meditations on your ruling passion, the virtues, and venial and mortal sin. Also, the month of October is dedicated to the holy angels and the Rosary.

Other special Feast Days dedicated to the angels include:
- *March 24 — St. Gabriel the Archangel,*
- *May 8 — Feast of St. Michael's Apparition on Mount Gargano in 492 A.D.,*
- *September 29 — the Holy Archangels,*
- *October 2 — the Guardian Angels,*
- *October 24 — St. Raphael the Archangel.*

The holy angels have always been a special part of my life. Among my earliest childhood recollections is a devotion to my Guardian Angel. I remember each night I'd only sleep on half of my twin bed so my Guardian Angel could have the other half. I was no more than 5 years old and told no one of my nightly routine.

"St. Matthew Writing his Gospel and an Angel" by Carlo Dolci (1670). Courtesy Wikimedia Commons.

The appearance of a Guardian Angel is also part of my family's history. My mother's sister, 8-year-old Ernestine, was bedridden due to a heart condition.

One morning, my mother was in the room holding her up while their older sister Nancy arranged the blankets at the foot of Ernestine's bed. My grandmother was nearby.

Suddenly, Ernestine became very animated, exclaiming, "Look, look! I can see Nancy's Guardian Angel!"

Everyone turned to each other, not understanding or knowing what to do. They asked questions. Ernestine described the angel as very beautiful, bright white and translucent.

She said the angel was blond, had no wings and was tall as Nancy, who was a teenager. She said the angel was following right alongside Nancy, helping her as she tucked the blankets underneath the edge of Ernestine's bed.

Ernestine was mesmerized by the sight, which vanished rapidly. The others present, who knew that Ernestine was very ill, took this as a sign that God would be taking Ernestine soon. A few days later, Ernestine died in her sleep. This incident has always been among my family's recollections, and I remember hearing about it since my youth.

Many of the images I've selected for this book involve the holy angels interacting with people, such as in visions and apparitions to the saints. My purpose is to offer examples of angels as distinct and real beings which have appeared to people.

There is a popular belief which holds that when people die, they become angels in Heaven. However the Catholic *Catechism* states that angels are spiritual beings which are entirely different from human beings. Although humans have immortal spiritual souls, which are glorified in Heaven, human souls are unique and do not alter their special nature to become something else.

I hope you find the prayers in this collection helpful in your spiritual journey.

— *Marie Noël*

CHAPTER 1: GOD THE FATHER, SON & BLESSED TRINITY

"Eternal Blessing" by Raphael (1507). Courtesy Wikimedia Commons.

"I saw an angel very near me, towards my left side, in bodily form, which is not usual with me; for though angels are often represented to me, it is only in my mental vision. This angel appeared rather small than large, and very beautiful. His face was so shining that he seemed to be one of those highest angels called seraphs, who look as if all on fire with divine love. He had in his hands a long golden dart; at the end of the point I thought there was a little fire. And I felt him thrust it several times through my heart. ...And when he drew it out, I thought it...left me wholly on fire with a great love of God."

—St. Teresa of Avila,
Mystic & Doctor of the Church,
on the piercing of her heart by an angel
(commemorated August 27 by the Carmelites)

*"An Angel Appears to Balaam" by Gustav Jaeger (1808-1871).
Courtesy Wikimedia Commons.*

Short Prayer for Angelic Assistance

O God, who in your providence were pleased to send your holy angels to keep watch over us, grant that we may always be defended and shielded by them and rejoice in their companionship. Through Christ our Lord. Amen.

Prayer for Angelic Ministries
(from 400-461 A.D.)

O God, who orders things in Heaven and earth alike for the assistance of mankind, we ask you that while we are laboring in the lower part of the universe, you would mercifully refresh us by the protection of your ministers from above, through Jesus Christ our Lord. Amen.

"Eternal Blessing by God the Father" by Pietro Perugino (circa 1512-1523).
Courtesy Wikimedia Commons.

Protection of Your Home

Hear us, O Holy Lord, Almighty Father, eternal God, and send your holy angel from Heaven to guard, cherish, protect, visit, and defend all who live in this house. Through Christ our Lord. Amen.

Another Prayer to Safeguard Your Home

O Lord, we ask you to visit this home and drive far from it all snares of the enemy. Let your holy angels dwell in it to preserve us in peace. Let your blessing be always upon us. Through Christ our Lord. Amen.

Prayer for Perseverance

O God, you have made blessed Michael, your Archangel, victorious over the proud Lucifer and all the wicked spirits. We ask you that, combating under the Cross and ever adopting St.Michael's maxim, *"Who is like unto God,"* we may be victorious over all our enemies, and be delivered from all evils. Regulate our lives according to your will and Commandments. Through Jesus Christ our Lord. Amen.

Blessed Sacrament: Offering of Guard of Honor of the Sacred Heart of Jesus

(Holy Hour devotion also called the Association of Presence to the Heart of Jesus)

Patrons for Each Hour

- *1 o'clock*— St. Joseph & all saints.
- *2 o'clock*—All just souls on earth.
- *3 o'clock*—Seraphim.
- *4 o'clock*—Cherubim.
- *5 o'clock*—Thrones.
- *6 o'clock*—Dominations.
- *7 o'clock*—Virtues.
- *8 o'clock*—Powers.
- *9 o'clock*—Principalities.
- *10 o'clock*—Archangels.
- *11 o'clock*—All angels.
- *12 o'clock*—Blessed Virgin Mary.

Dearest Jesus, my sweetest Savior, I offer you this Holy Hour of guard, during which, in union with *[here name the patrons of your hour]*, I desire to love and glorify you, and, above all, to console your adorable heart for the forgetfulness and ingratitude of mankind.

Accept, I ask you, for this end, all my thoughts, words, actions, and sufferings; above all, receive my heart, which I give you without reserve, asking you to consume it in the fire of your pure love.

May the Sacred Heart of Jesus be loved everywhere. O my Jesus, I desire to love you through this hour for all those hearts who don't love you. Amen.

"Angels Adoring the Blessed Sacrament" by anonymous. Courtesy Wikimedia Commons.

"St. Michael the Archangel in Battle" by Gerard David (1510). Courtesy Wikimedia Commons.

Lorica of St. Patrick

[also known as St. Patrick's Breastplate, composed by St. Patrick (387-461 A.D.) prior to his victory over paganism]

I arise today through a mighty strength, the invocation of the Trinity, through a belief in the threeness, through a confession of the oneness of the Creator of creation.

I arise today through the strength of Christ's birth with his Baptism, through the strength of his crucifixion with his burial, through the strength of his resurrection with his ascension, through the strength of his descent for the judgment of Doom.

I arise today through the strength of the love of Cherubim, in obedience of Angels, in the service of Archangels, in hope of resurrection to meet with reward, in prayers of patriarchs, in predictions of prophets, in preachings of apostles, in faiths of confessors, in innocence of holy virgins, in deeds of righteous men.

I arise today through the strength of Heaven: light of sun, radiance of moon, splendor of fire, speed of lightning, swiftness of wind, depth of sea, stability of earth, firmness of rock.

I arise today through God's strength to pilot me, God's might to uphold me, God's wisdom to guide me, God's eye to look before me, God's ear to hear me, God's word to speak for me, God's hand to guard me, God's way to lie before me, God's shield to protect me, and God's host to save me from snares of devils, from temptations of vices, from everyone who shall wish me ill, afar and near, alone and in a multitude.

I summon today all these powers between me and those evils, against every cruel merciless power that may oppose my body and soul, against incantations of false prophets, against black laws of pagandom, against false laws of heretics, against craft of idolatry, against spells, against every knowledge that corrupts man's body and soul.

Christ shield me today against poison, against burning, against drowning, against wounding, so that there may come to me abundance of reward,
Christ with me,
Christ before me,
Christ behind me,
Christ in me,
Christ beneath me,
Christ above me,
Christ on my right,
Christ on my left,
Christ when I lie down,

"Throne of Grace" by unknown (circa 1345). Courtesy Wikimedia Commons.

Christ when I sit down,
Christ when I arise,
Christ in the heart of every man who thinks of me,
Christ in the mouth of everyone who speaks of me,
Christ in every eye that sees me, and Christ in every ear that
hears me.

I arise today through a mighty strength, the invocation of the
Trinity, through a belief in the threeness, through a confession
of the oneness of the Creator of Creation. Amen.

*"Angels Holding the Four Winds" by Matthias Gerung (circa 1530–1532).
Courtesy Wikimedia Commons.*

Holy Trinity Novena

Heavenly Father, creator of Heaven and earth, I praise and thank you, not only because you created the visible world, but also because you have created the heavens and called the numberless spirits into being. You created them most splendidly, endowing them with power and understanding, and pouring out upon them the riches of your grace. I praise and thank you for having showered these blessings upon the good angels, especially upon my Guardian Angel, and for having rewarded them with eternal glory. Now they surround your throne forever, singing jubilantly:

  • *Holy, holy, holy, Lord, God of hosts! Heaven and earth are full of your glory. Hosanna in the highest!*

Eternal Son of God, I honor you as the king of the angels. Yet you were pleased to dwell among us. You were the faithful companion and constant leader of the chosen people. By your incarnation you became the ambassador of our heavenly father and the messenger of the great decree of our redemption. For your greater glory, loving king of the angels, I wish to praise and honor your servants, the Holy Angels, especially my own Guardian Angel. In union with these Holy Angels I adore and revere you as my savior and my God.

Holy Spirit, divine artist, finger of God's right hand, by your power and love the hosts of the angels were brought into being to adore and serve God. They do so with constant fidelity and ready obedience. They carry out your commands with fervent love and holy zeal. Divine Spirit, you also created us in your likeness and made of our souls your living temples. I thank you for having given us your Holy Angels to help, protect, and guide us that we may persevere in your grace throughout life's journey and safely reach our heavenly home. Help me to be attentive to their guidance that I may do your holy will perfectly and, at the same time, find true happiness in this life and in the next. Amen.

Most Holy Trinity, Father, Son, and Holy Spirit, in honor of the Holy Angels, I ask you to grant my special request if it be your holy will. *(Mention your request.)*

O all you Holy Angels, who contemplate unceasingly the uncreated beauty of the divinity, we present and offer to you this novena not only as a means of obtaining favors, but also as a reparation for our past ingratitude, and that of all men.

Accept it, O amiable spirits, in union with the love and devotion of such saints as were especially devoted to you, and obtain for us the grace to spend this life fervently that it may be the commencement of that blessed life that we hope to live forever with you in Heaven.

O God, who with wonderful order has regulated the functions of angels and men, grant that those who always assist before your throne in Heaven may defend our lives here on earth, through Jesus Christ, your son, our lord, who lives and reigns with you, in the unity of the Holy Spirit, one God, world without end. Amen.

"Transverberation of St. Teresa of Jesus" by Josefa de Obidos (1672). Courtesy Wikimedia Commons.

1st Day: Ardent Seraphim, you who dwell in the eternal home of love, unceasingly absorbed in the rays of the sun of justice, we beg you in virtue of the divine blood, to enkindle in our hearts that holy fire with which you are consumed.

    • *St. Michael the Archangel, and all the Holy Angels, protect us in our combats that we may not perish in the tremendous judgment of God. Amen.*

2nd Day: Bright Cherubim, you who are allowed a deeper insight into God's secrets, dispel the darkness of our souls, and in virtue of the divine blood, give that supernatural light to our eyes that will enable us to understand the truths of salvation.

    • *St. Michael the Archangel, and all the Holy Angels, protect us in our combats that we may not perish in the tremendous judgment of God. Amen.*

3rd Day: Sublime Thrones, dazzling in your beauty, upon whom rests the Almighty and who convey his commands to the inferior angels, obtain for us in virtue of the divine blood, peace with God, with our neighbor and with ourselves.

    • *St. Michael the Archangel, and all the Holy Angels, protect us in our combats that we may not perish in the tremendous judgment of God. Amen.*

"The Vision of Ezekiel" by Raphael (1518). Courtesy Wikimedia Commons.

4th Day: Supreme Dominations, you who have the authority over all angelic choirs, and are charged with the execution of God's orders, rule over our minds and hearts, and in virtue of the divine blood, help us to know and faithfully to accomplish the will of God.

• *St. Michael the Archangel, and all the Holy Angels, protect us in our combats that we may not perish in the tremendous judgment of God. Amen.*

5th Day: Invincible Powers, whose mission it is to remove the obstacles to the divine will and overcome its enemies, defend us against the attacks of the world, the flesh and the devil, and in virtue of the divine blood, render us victorious in our combats against this triple power.

• *St. Michael the Archangel, and all the Holy Angels, protect us in our combats that we may not perish in the tremendous judgment of God. Amen.*

6th Day: Heavenly Virtues, who watch over the harmony of the material creation, you whose name signifies strength, have pity on our weakness, and obtain for us in virtue of the divine blood the grace to bear with patience the trials of this life.

• *St. Michael the Archangel, and all the Holy Angels, protect us in our combats that we may not perish in the tremendous judgment of God. Amen.*

7th Day: Sovereign Principalities, you who are the princes of nations, we ask you to guard our country effectively, that it may realize God's designs in its regard. Govern our souls and bodies, and in virtue of the divine blood, obtain for us our attainment of eternal life.

• *St. Michael the Archangel, and all the Holy Angels, protect us in our combats that we may not perish in the tremendous judgment of God. Amen.*

8th Day: Most noble Archangels, you who under the command of St. Michael guard and protect the church, deliver her from internal and external enemies. Watch over all the children of the church, and in virtue of the divine blood, obtain for us the grace to live and die with faith in our hearts so that we may be eternally united with Jesus Christ, our lord.

• *St. Michael the Archangel, and all the Holy Angels, protect us in our combats that we may not perish in the tremendous judgment of God. Amen.*

9th Day: Most holy Angels, you whose zeal for the interests of God, wherever they need to be defended, carries you through the universe more rapidly than lightning, protect his cause in our souls, and in virtue of the divine blood, obtain for us the grace of final perseverance.

• *St. Michael the Archangel, and all the Holy Angels, protect us in our combats that we may not perish in the tremendous judgment of God. Amen.*

Closing Prayer

O most glorious prince, Michael, the Archangel, remember us, here and everywhere, and always pray to the son of God for us.

"The Expulsion of Adam and Eve from Paradise" by Benjamin West (1791). Courtesy Wikimedia Commons.

I will praise you, O God, in the sight of your angels. I will adore you in your holy temple, and I will confess your name. O God, who has in an admirable order disposed the ministry of angels and of men, grant in your goodness that our life on earth may be protected by those who in Heaven always stand before your throne, ready to assist you and to do your will.

Bless the lord, all you angels. You who are mighty in strength and do his will, intercede for me at the throne of God. By your unceasing watchfulness protect me from every danger of soul and body.

Obtain for me the grace of final perseverance, so that after this life I may be admitted to your glorious company and with you may sing the praises of God for all eternity.

All you holy Angels and Archangels, Thrones and Dominations, Principalities and Powers and Virtues of Heaven, Cherubim and Seraphim, and especially you, my dear Guardian Angel, intercede for me and obtain for me the special favor I now ask. *(Mention your request.)* Amen.

"Apparition of the Eucharist to St. Paschal Baylon, patron of Eucharistic congresses &
associations" by Bernardo López (1811). Courtesy Wikimedia Commons.

Blessed Sacrament Prayer to the Saints and Angels

O Divine Jesus! I adore you in this mystery of faith and love, in which by your exceedingly great kindness and charity, you daily renew the sacrifice of yourself for us. Destroy in me all that is displeasing to your pure eyes, so I may be as a living offering, pleasing and acceptable before the throne of your love!

To you, O holy Virgin, I have recourse in this happy moment when duty calls me before the Divine Lamb, my dearest

Jesus, ever present in this most Blessed Sacrament, to pay him my tribute of praise and adoration. Oh, obtain for me a heart penetrated with profound humility, lively faith, and ardent love, that during this hour of adoration, I may have deep sorrow for my sins and those of the whole world.

Glorious St. Joseph, first adorer of the sacred humanity of my Savior, adorn my soul with your own virtues and merits, and obtain for me the divine favor now and at the hour of my death.

Angels of Heaven who surround this tabernacle, I unite my humble adorations to your seraphic ardors. Oh, that I could render to this Lord of glory an adoration and love like yours.

How great is my consolation and happiness, O my Divine Savior in finding myself at this moment in your sacred presence, kneeling at the foot of your altar, and speaking to you alone. How have I desired to be here so I may pour out my whole heart before you.

You are my repose, my life, my happiness, and my joy. Absent from you, I am, as it were, apart from my only end and center; near you, I wish to forget the whole world, and all created things.

Banish from my mind every distracting, vain, and frivolous thought that keeps you away from me; and erase from my heart all such languor, tepidity, and negligence, as may render my homages of praise unworthy. Let me be occupied with you alone, adoring your almighty greatness, asking favors, and lamenting my many transgressions and miseries.

O my God, I ask your abundant mercies, fervor in your service, deliverance from sin, resignation under sufferings, conformity to your will, perfect abandonment into the hands of your Divine Providence, and above all, I ask you to give me your love. Amen.

"The Baptism of Christ" by Adam Elsheimer (circa 1559). Courtesy Wikimedia Commons.

The Divine Praises

(by Fr. Luigi Felici in 1797 to counter blasphemy & profanity*)

Blessed be God.

Blessed be his holy name.

Blessed be Jesus Christ, true God and true man.

Blessed be the name of Jesus.

Blessed be his most Sacred Heart.

Blessed be his most Precious Blood.

Blessed be Jesus in the most Holy Sacrament of the Altar.

Blessed be the Holy Spirit, the Paraclete.

Blessed be the great mother of God, Mary most holy.

Blessed be her holy and Immaculate Conception.

Blessed be her glorious Assumption.

Blessed be the name of Mary, virgin and mother.

Blessed be St. Joseph, her most chaste spouse.

Blessed be God in his angels and in his saints. Amen.

* Expanded in 1801 by Pope Pius VII.

"Triumph of Christ with Angels and Cherubs" by Bernardino Lanino (circa 1550). Courtesy Wikimedia Commons.

Prayer For Travelers

O Almighty and merciful God, who has commissioned your angels to guide and protect us, command them to be our companions from our departure until our return; to clothe us with their invisible protection; to keep from us all danger of collision, of fire, of explosion, of falls and bruises, and finally, having preserved us from all evil, and especially from sin, to guide us to our heavenly home. Through Jesus Christ, our Lord. Amen.

Te Deum
(from the 4th century)

O God, we praise you, and acknowledge you to be the supreme Lord.

Everlasting Father, all the earth worships you.

All the Angels, the heavens and all angelic powers,

All the Cherubim and Seraphim, continuously cry to you:

Holy, holy, holy, Lord God of Hosts!

"Tobias Meets the Archangel Raphael" by Andrea Vaccaro (circa 1640). Courtesy
Wikimedia Commons.

Heaven and earth are full of the majesty of your glory.

The glorious choir of apostles, wonderful company of
prophets, and white-robed army of martyrs, praise you.

The Holy Church throughout the world acknowledges you.
The Father of infinite majesty; your adorable, true and only
Son; also the Holy Spirit, the comforter.

O Christ, you are the king of glory! You are the everlasting
son of the Father. When you took it upon yourself to deliver
man, you didn't disdain the Virgin's womb. Having overcome
the sting of death, you opened the Kingdom of Heaven to all
believers. You sit at the right hand of God in the glory of the
Father. We believe that you will come to be our judge.

We, therefore, beg you to help your servants whom you
have redeemed with your precious blood. Let them be
numbered with your saints in everlasting glory.

"The Throne of Grace" by unknown (circa 1410). Courtesy Wikimedia Commons.

- *Save your people, O Lord, and bless your inheritance! Govern them, and raise them up forever.*
- *Everyday we thank you. And we praise your name forever and ever.*
- *O Lord, keep us from sin this day.*
- *Have mercy on us, O Lord, have mercy on us. Let your mercy, O Lord, be upon us, for we have hoped in you.*
- *O Lord, in you I put my trust; let me never be put to shame.*

Prayer for You & Your Friends
(from the 11th Century)

O Lord God, Father Almighty, who has promised rewards to the just and pardon to the penitent, who wills not the death of sinners nor has pleasure in the destruction of any who die, I humbly ask you, for the sake of the most Holy

Mary, Mother of God, and all your saints, and your own mercy, grant me the remission of all my sins, and bring me to that penitence by which you saved David, looked graciously upon Peter as he wept, and cleansed Mary Magdalene.

O Lord Jesus Christ, cast out of my heart all things that offend you; and pour into me such love that I may be enabled perfectly to love and fear you, and neither to think nor desire anything except what is pleasing to you, O Lord.

I ask you, Blessed Virgin Mary, temple of the Lord, sanctuary of the Holy Ghost; I also ask you holy Archangels Michael, Gabriel, and Raphael, and all our appointed guardian angels, and the Nine Angelic Orders, to intercede for me: also Peter, Paul, Andrew, John, and all apostles, martyrs, confessors, virgins, saints, and elect of God, to protect me when I come before the Tribunal of the Eternal King to be judged.

I commend to you, most loving Jesus Christ, all who love or care for me, all who give me pitying aid, all who are indebted to me, or related to me. And likewise for my enemies, I ask that you would turn them to peace and cause them to attain true penitence.

I ask you, O Lord Jesus Christ, mercifully to remember all those who care for me, and who have commended themselves to my unworthy prayers, and who have done me any charity or kindness; as well as all who are connected to me by relationship, friendship, or the bonds of faith (whether they be still in the body or have departed this life) and visit them, that they, faithfully serving you, may be defended from all adversities.

Grant to them and me deliverance from all punishment, and bring us to everlasting rest. And this I earnestly ask, that whenever the day of my death shall come, you yourself, who gives judgment against the accusers, will show me divine mercy, who are blessed forever and ever. Amen.

CHAPTER 2: MARY, QUEEN OF ANGELS

"Assumption of the Virgin" by Guido Reni (1580). Courtesy Wikimedia Commons.

Mary is Queen in her service to God for humanity, a Queen of love who gives the gift of herself to God to enter into the plan of man's salvation. So how does Mary exercise this queenship of service and love? By watching over us, her children who turn to her in prayer, to thank or ask for her motherly protection and heavenly help, perhaps after having lost our way, or when we are oppressed by suffering or anguish because of the sorrowful and harrowing vicissitudes of life.

"The Annunciation" by Benvenuto Tisi da Garofalo (1528).
Courtesy Wikimedia Commons.

For centuries she has been invoked as the celestial Queen of Heaven. The rhythm of these ancient invocations and daily prayers help us understand that the Blessed Virgin, as our Mother beside her Son Jesus in the glory of Heaven, is always with us in the daily events of our life. The title "Queen" is a title of trust, joy and love. And we know that the One who holds a part of the world's destinies in her hand is good, that she loves us and helps us in our difficulties.

—*Pope Benedict XVI*

Prayer to the Queen of Angels
(by St. Frances of Rome, 1384-1440 A.D.)

Hail Daughter and handmaid of the Most High King and spouse of the Holy Ghost; we ask that you, with St. Michael the Archangel, and all the powers of Heaven, and all the saints, intercede for us with your most beloved son, our lord and master, who with the same Father and Holy Ghost, lives and reigns forever and ever. Amen.

*"Madonna and Child with Angels" by Hans Memling (circa 1479).
Courtesy The National Gallery of Art.*

The Hail Mary (Angelic Salutation)

Hail Mary, full of grace, our Lord is with thee, blessed art thou among women, and blessed is the fruit of thy womb, Jesus. Holy Mary, Mother of God, pray for us sinners, now, and at the hour of our death. Amen.

The Angelus

The Angel of the Lord declared to Mary. And she conceived of the Holy Spirit.

• *Hail Mary, full of grace, our Lord is with thee, blessed art thou among women, and blessed is the fruit of thy womb, Jesus. Holy Mary, Mother of God, pray for us sinners, now, and at the hour of our death. Amen.*

Behold the handmaid of the Lord: Be it done unto me according to your word.

• *Hail Mary...*

"The Immaculate Conception" by Martino Altomonte (1719). Courtesy Wikimedia Commons.

And the Word was made Flesh: And dwelt among us.
 • *Hail Mary...*
Pray for us, O Holy Mother of God that we may be made worthy of the promises of Christ.

Let Us Pray

Pour forth, we ask you, O Lord, your grace into our hearts; that we, to whom the incarnation of Christ, your son, was made known by the message of an angel, may by his passion and cross be brought to the glory of his resurrection, through the same Christ our Lord. Amen.

"Madonna & Child with Angels" by Jan Provost (1510). Courtesy Wikimedia Commons.

PRAYER TO OUR LADY, QUEEN OF ANGELS

August Queen of Heaven, sovereign Mistress of the Angels, who did receive from the beginning the mission and the power to crush the serpent's head, we ask you to send your holy angels, that under your command and by your power, they may pursue the evil spirits, encounter them on every side, resist their bold attacks, and drive them into the abyss of woe.

Most holy Mother, send your angels to defend us and to drive the cruel enemy from us. All you holy angels and archangels, help and defend us. O good and tender Mother! You shall ever be our love and our hope. Holy Angels and Archangels, keep and defend us. Amen.

"Virgin of Humility" by Fra Angelico (1435). Courtesy Wikimedia Commons.

THREE OFFERINGS IN HONOR OF THE BLESSED VIRGIN MARY

1. Holiest Virgin, with all my heart I venerate you above all the angels and saints in paradise as the daughter of the eternal Father, and to you I consecrate my soul and all its powers.

• *Hail Mary, full of grace, our Lord is with thee, blessed art thou among women, and blessed is the fruit of thy womb, Jesus. Holy Mary, Mother of God, pray for us sinners, now, and at the hour of our death. Amen*

2. Holiest Virgin, with all my heart I venerate you above all the angels and saints in paradise as the Mother of the only-begotten son, and to you I consecrate my body with all its senses.

• *Hail Mary...*

3. Holiest Virgin, with all my heart I venerate you above all the angels and saints in paradise as the spouse of the Holy Ghost, and to you I consecrate my heart and all its affections, praying you to obtain for me from the ever-blessed Trinity all the graces which I need for my salvation.

• *Hail Mary...*

FOR THE REIGN OF THE SACRED HEART

O Mary Immaculate, great Queen of Heaven and earth and our gentle advocate, we beg you to intercede for us. Pray to God to send St. Michael and the holy Angels to ward off all the obstacles contrary to the reign of the Sacred Heart in our souls, our families, our country and in the whole world.

And you, O holy Michael, prince of the heavenly hosts, from our hearts we beg you to come to our aid.

Defend us against the rage of Satan. Through the Divine power bestowed on you by God, after securing victory for the Church here below, guide our souls to our eternal home. St. Michael, first champion of the Kingship of Christ, pray for us! Amen.

"Coronation of the Madonna and Child" in The Moulins Triptych by the Master of Moulins (circa 1498). Courtesy Wikimedia Commons.

NOVENA PRAYER IN HONOR OF OUR QUEEN OF THE ANGELS

O Mary, ever blessed Virgin, Mother of God, Queen of the angels and of the saints, I salute you with the most profound veneration and devotion.

"Assumption of the Virgin" by Sano di Petri (between 1448 and 1452). Courtesy Wikimedia Commons.

I renew the consecration of myself and all that I have to you. I thank you for your maternal protection and the many blessings I have received through your wondrous mercy and most powerful intercession. In all my needs I have recourse to you with utmost confidence.

O Help of Christians, O Mother of Mercy, I ask you now to hear my prayer, and to obtain for me of your Divine Son the favor that I request in this novena.

Obtain for me, also, dearest Mother, the grace that I may imitate you and become more like you in the practice of the virtues of humility, obedience, purity, poverty, submission to the will of God, and charity.

Protect me in my life, guard and guide me in dangers, direct me in moments of confusion, lead me in the way of perfection, and assist me in the hour of my death, that I may come to Jesus, and with you bless him and love him eternally in Heaven. Amen.

NOVENA FOR THE ASSUMPTION OF THE VIRGIN MARY

Majestic Queen of Heaven and Mistress of the Angels, you received from God the power and command to crush the head of Satan.

Therefore, we humbly beg of you, send forth the legions of Heaven, that under your command they may seek out all evil spirits, engage them everywhere in battle, curb their pride, and hurl them back into the pit of hell. *"Who is like unto God?"*

With firm confidence we present ourselves before you, our most loving Mother, afflicted and troubled as we are. We ask you to grant this petition, if it is according to the will of God and good for our salvation. *(Mention your request.)*

Good and tender Mother, you shall ever be our hope and the object of our love.

Mother of God, send forth the Holy Angels to defend us and drive far from us the cruel foe.

Holy Angels and Archangels, defend and keep us. Amen.

"Song of the Angels" by William-Adolphe Bouguereau (1881). Courtesy Wikimedia Commons.

Litany of Our Lady of the Angels
(from Franciscan prayer for August 2, Feast of Our Lady of the Angels)

Antiphon:

Under your title so dear to St. Francis, our Blessed Lady of Angels, we hail you! Give us your aid so that our lives become more seraphic and we may never fail you.

- *The Angel of the Lord declared unto Mary:*
- *And she conceived by the Holy Ghost.*

Lord have mercy on us.
Christ have mercy on us.
Christ hear us.
Christ graciously hear us.
Holy Mary, Mother of God, *pray for us.*
Holy Mary, Our Lady of the Angels, *pray for us.*
Our Lady, to whom the Father sent his messenger, *pray for us.*
Our Lady, before whom knelt the Archangel Gabriel, *pray for us.*
Our Lady, consenting to become the Mother of God, *pray for us.*
Our Lady, whose Angel Michael defends the people of God, *pray for us.*
Our Lady, whose Angel Raphael guides us safely on our journey, *pray for us.*
Our Lady, whose angels serve as our guardians, *pray for us.*
Our Lady, whose angels bore your little house of Nazareth to Loreto, *pray for us.*
Our Lady, whose angels carried your image to Genezzano, *pray for us.*
Our Lady, whose chapel of Portiuncula, the gift of holy Benedict, was the cradle of the Franciscan Order, *pray for us.*
Our Lady, for whose chapel of St. Mary of the Angels you obtained plenary favors from your son and from his vicar, *pray for us.*
Our Lady, whose little poor man is hailed as the seraphic father St. Francis, *pray for us.*

Our Lady, who caused St. Francis to be given the vacated throne from which the rebellious angel Lucifer was cast down, *pray for us.*

Our Lady, at whose Assumption hosts of angels flew heavenward in your company, *pray for us.*

Our Lady, queen of Thrones and Dominations, Principalities and the whole angelic Court of Heaven, *pray for us.*

Our Lady, ever surrounded by myriad seraphs, *pray for us.*

Holy Mary, Our Lady of the Angels, *pray for us.*

Holy Mary, Mother of God and our Mother, *pray for us.*

- *Pray for us, Queen of the Angelic Hosts,*
- *That we may be made worthy of the promises of Christ.*

Let Us Pray

O God, who permits us annually to celebrate anew the dedication day of the chapel of Our Lady of the Angels, graciously hear the prayers of your people and grant that all who enter that chapel or another as representing it, to ask mercy and graces, may rejoice in the plenary answer to their prayers. Through Christ Our Lord.

O God, who through your most holy mother, exalted above the angel choirs, has called all people of good will to receive your mercy: grant to us, who commemorate the consecration of her chapel, that we may be freed of our sins and obtain the fullness of grace, until at last we attain the company of her blessed angels and the joy of her heavenly mansion. Who lives and reigns world without end.

Our Holy Queen of all of God's angels, pray for us, your children. Jesus, Mary and Joseph, bless our hearts. Amen.

CHAPTER 3: GUARDIAN ANGELS

"A Soul Taken Away by an Angel" by Jean-Léon Gérôme (1853).
Courtesy Wikimedia Commons.

"In the hours when you seem to be alone and abandoned, do not complain of not having a friendly soul to whom you can unburden yourself and in whom you can confide your sorrows. For pity's sake, do not forget this invisible companion, always present to listen to you, always ready to console you. ...Invoke your Guardian Angel that he illuminate you and will guide you. God has given him to you for this reason. Therefore use him!"

—St. Padre Pio,
famed for his devotion to & reliance on
Guardian Angels

"*St. Agatha Attended by St. Peter and an Angel in Prison,*" *by Alessandro Turchi*
(1615). Courtesy The Walters Art Museum.

Aspiration

O my dear Angel Guardian, keep me from the misfortune of offending God. Amen.

Morning Prayer

O my holy angel guardian, I thank you for having so carefully watched over me this night. I ask you and all the other holy angels to guard me during this day and until the end of my life. Amen.

Night Prayer

Holy angel guardian and all you saints of God, protect me this night and preserve me from all evil. Amen.

*"An Angel Fighting for a Soul" by Alexey Tyranov (circa 1800s).
Courtesy Wikimedia Commons.*

Prayer for the Dying

My holy angel guardian, stand by me and protect me in this hour; do not let the enemy of my soul have any power over me. O my holy angel guardian, take charge of my soul and lead it into the presence of God. Amen.

Memorare to Our Angel Guardian

Remember O holy Angel, you whom Jesus, the Eternal Truth, assures us does "rejoice more at the conversion of one sinner than at the perseverance of many just."

Encouraged therefore, I humbly ask you to receive me as your child and to make me a cause of true joy for you. Do not, O blessed Spirit, reject my petition, but graciously hear and grant it. Amen.

To Our Guardian Angel
(by St. Gertrude, 1256-1301 A.D.)

O most holy Angel of God, appointed by him to be my guardian, I give you thanks for all the benefits which you have ever bestowed on me in body and in soul. I praise and glorify you that you assist me with such patient fidelity, and defend me against all the assaults of my enemies.

Blessed be the hour in which you were assigned me for my guardian, my defender, and my patron. In acknowledgment and return of all your loving ministries to me from my youth onwards, I offer you the infinitely precious and noble heart of Jesus, and firmly purpose to obey you from now on, and most faithfully to serve my God. Amen.

"A Guardian Angel" by Andrea Pozzo (circa 1685-1694).
Courtesy Wikimedia Commons.

Prayer for Travelers

My holy angel guardian, ask the Lord to bless the journey which I undertake, that it may be good for the health of my soul and body; that I may reach its end; and returning safe and sound, I may find everyone at home in good health and my home kept safe. I ask you to guard, guide, and preserve us. Amen.

Prayer for those Afflicted with Spiritual Lukewarmness

My God! I am truly nothing, and I can do nothing. I do not know even what to say to you; but listen to the heart of your Divine Son; I offer to you all he said in his fervent prayers.

Holy Angel, my guide and friend, pray for me.

Holy Angel, my counselor and intercessor, pray for me

Holy Angel, my protector and comforter, pray for me.

My good Angel, obtain for me obedience to all your inspirations.

My dear Angel, you who always stands before the Lord, love him for me, adore him for me, and keep me always attentive to his holy presence. Amen.

"Vision of Cornelius the Centurion" by Gerbrand van den Eeckhout (1664).
Courtesy The Walters Art Museum.

For Angelic Guidance or Direction

Dear wise and holy angels of God, I seek your advice and ask you for light and direction.

Let me know the will of God and how I am supposed to act.

Lift my prayers to God's altar in Heaven and intercede for me.

Let your divine light shine on me, and do not abandon me to my own darkness. Amen.

"Angels escort St. Catherine of Alexandria to Heaven after her Martyrdom" by Heinrich Mücke (1836). Courtesy Wikimedia Commons.

Recommendation to One's Guardian Angel for a Happy Death
(by St. Charles Borromeo, 1538-1584 A.D.)

My good angel, I know not when or how I shall die. It is possible I may be carried off suddenly, and that before my last sigh I may be deprived of all intelligence. Yet how many things I would wish to say to God on the threshold of eternity. In the full freedom of my will today, I come to ask you to speak for me at that fearful moment.

You will say to God, O my good angel, that I wish to die in the faith of the true one, holy, Catholic, and Apostolic Church in which all the saints since Jesus Christ have died. I ask the grace of sharing in the infinite merits of my Redeemer, and I desire to die in pressing to my lips the cross that was bathed in his blood. That I detest all of my sins because they displease him, and that I pardon through love of him all my enemies as I wish myself to be pardoned.

"Guardian Angel" by Domenichino (1615). Courtesy Wikimedia Commons.

That I die willingly because he orders it and I throw myself with confidence into his adorable heart awaiting all his mercy. That in my inexpressible desire to go to Heaven, I am disposed to suffer everything it may please his sovereign justice to inflict on me.

That I love him before all things, above all things and for his own sake; that I wish and hope to love him with the elect, his angels and the Blessed Mother during all eternity.

Do not refuse, O my angel, to be my interpreter with God, and to protest to him that these are my sentiments and my will. Amen.

A Prayer to Our Angel Guardian
(1600s French prayer)

O most faithful companion, whom God has appointed to watch over me, my guide and protector, ever at my side, I offer you thanks for your love, constancy, and innumerable benefits.

You watch over me in sleep, comfort me in sorrow, raise me when I fall, keep away dangers, prepare me for the future, withdraw me from sin, urge me to do good, move me to do penance, and reconcile me with my God. Don't leave me, I ask you.

Encourage me in adversity, restrain me in prosperity, protect me in dangers, and assist me in temptations so I don't give into them. Offer to the Divine Majesty all my prayers and sighs and works, and obtain for me the grace to die in the friendship of God, and to enter into life eternal. Amen.

Another Prayer to Our Guardian Angel

O Angel of God, my guardian, enlighten, guard, protect, and govern me, who has been given to you by the heavenly mercy. Amen.

Angel of God
(Angele Dei)

Angel of God, my guardian dear, to whom his love commits me here; ever this (day, night) be at my side, to light and guard, to rule and guide. Amen.

"Guardian Angel Watches over Sleeping Child" by Melchior Paul von Deschwanden (1859). Courtesy Wikimedia Commons.

To My Good Angel Guardian

O Angel of God, my blessed protector and most amiable guardian, to whom God entrusted from the moment of my birth, join me in thanking the Almighty for having given me a friend, an instructor, an advocate, and a guardian in you.

Accept, O most charitable guide, my fervent thanksgiving for all you have done for me, especially the charity with which you have accompanied me through life; for your joy when I was purified in the waters of Baptism, and for your anxious care in watching over the treasures of my innocence. You know the numberless graces and favors that my Creator has given me through you, and the many dangers, both spiritual and temporal, from which you have saved me.

You know how often you deplored my sins, moved me to repentance, and interceded with God for my pardon.

*"St. Francis and the Angel" by Orazio Gentileschi (circa 1612).
Courtesy Wikimedia Commons.*

I most earnestly ask you, O protecting Spirit, to continue your zealous efforts for my eternal interest; to watch over me, direct my inexperience, fortify my weakness, shield me from the numerous dangers of the world, and obtain by your powerful prayers that my life may be shortened rather than that I should live to commit a mortal sin.

Conduct me safely through this world of sin and misery; watch over me at the hour of my death; and then, as the Angel Raphael conducted Tobias safely to his father, return with me to God who sent you so we may both bless him and praise his wonderful deeds in a happy eternity. Amen.

"The Angel and the Mother" by Louis Janmot (1854).
Courtesy Wikimedia Commons.

A Mother's Prayer to the Guardian Angels of Her Children

I humbly salute you, O you faithful, heavenly friends of my children! I give you heartfelt thanks for all the love and goodness you show them.

At some future day I shall, with thanks more worthy than I can give now, repay your care for them, and before the whole heavenly court acknowledge their indebtedness to your guidance and protection. Continue to watch over them. Provide for all their needs of body and soul.

Pray for me, for my husband, and my whole family, that we may all one day rejoice in your blessed company. Amen.

PRAYER TO ALL GUARDIAN ANGELS

O pure and happy spirits whom the Almighty selected to become the Angels and guardians of men! I most humbly kneel before you, to thank you for the charity and zeal with which you perform this duty.

O resplendent Spirits, who cannot avoid loving those whom Jesus eternally loved, permit me to address you on behalf of all those committed to your care, and to implore for them all a grateful sense of your many favors, and also the grace to profit by your charitable assistance.

O Angel of those happy infants, who as yet are spotless before God, I earnestly ask you to preserve their innocence.

O Angels of youth, conduct them, exposed to so many dangers, safely to the bosom of God, as Tobias was conducted back to his father.

O Angels of those who employ themselves to teach youths, animate them with your zeal and love, teach them to emulate your purity and incessant view of God, that they may worthily and successfully cooperate with the invisible Guardians of their young charges.

O Angels of the clergy "who have the eternal Gospel to preach to all nations," present their words, actions and intentions to God, and purify them in that fire of love with which you are consumed.

O Angels of the missionaries who have left their native land and all who were dear to them to preach the Gospel in foreign countries, protect them from the physical dangers which threaten them, and especially from the defilement of the corrupting spirit of the world; console them in their hours of depression and solitude and lead them to those souls who are in danger of dying without Baptism.

O Angels of unbelievers whom the true faith has never enlightened, intercede for them that they may at least open their hearts to the rays of grace, respond to the message delivered by God's missionaries, and acknowledge and adore the one true God.

O Angels of all who travel by air, land or water, be their guides and companions, protect them from all dangers of collision, of fire and explosion, and lead them safely to their destination.

O Guardian Angels of sinners, join me, I strongly ask you, in imploring their lasting conversion.

And you, O Guardian Angels of the sick, I ask you especially to help, console and implore the spirit of joy for all those who are deprived of health. Intercede for them that they may not succumb to despondency or lose by impatience the merits they can gain in carrying with resignation and joy the cross which Jesus Christ has laid upon them as a special token of his love.

O Angels of those people who at this moment struggle in the agonies of death, strengthen, encourage and defend them against the attacks of the infernal enemy.

O faithful guides, holy spirits, adorers of the divinity, Guardian Angels of all creatures, protect us all, teach us to love, to pray, and combat on earth, so that one day we may reach Heaven and there be happy there for all eternity. Amen.

"Apparition of an Angel to St. Roch" by Gaspar Dias (circa 1584).
Courtesy Wikimedia Commons.

Daily October Novena to the Holy Angels
(Oct. 2, Feast of the Guardian Angels)

O all you holy angels, who contemplate unceasingly the uncreated beauty of the divinity, in company with our ever-glorious Queen, we present and offer to you this novena, not only as a means of obtaining favors, but also as a reparation for our past ingratitude and that of all people. Accept our humble prayers, O amiable Spirits, in union with the love and devotion of the saints who were especially devout to you and obtain for us the grace to live good, happy lives which are the beginning of the joyful life we will share with you forever in Heaven. *(Mention your intentions.)*

"St. Cecilia and an Angel" by Carlo Saraceni (1610). Courtesy Wikimedia Commons.

Let Us Pray

O God, who with wonderful order has regulated the functions of angels and men, grant that those who always assist before your throne in Heaven may defend our lives here on earth, through Jesus Christ, your son, our Lord, who lives and reigns with you, in the unity of the Holy Ghost, one God, forever and ever. Amen.

Novena to Our Angel Guardian
(from the 1800s)

• *Glory be to the Father and to the Son and to the Holy Spirit. As it was in the beginning is now, and ever shall be, world without end. Amen.*

1st Day: O most powerful angel, you who are my guardian, I ask you obtain for me a sincere and lasting sorrow for my sins, and an implacable hatred against all sin, of any kind whatsoever, so that I may never offend my God.

• *Our Father, who art in Heaven, hallowed be thy Name, thy kingdom come, thy will be done, on earth as it is in Heaven. Give us this day our daily bread, and forgive us our trespasses, as we forgive those who trespass against us. And lead us not into temptation, but deliver us from evil. Amen.*

• *Hail Mary, full of grace, the Lord is with thee: blessed art thou amongst women, and blessed is the fruit of thy womb, Jesus. Holy Mary, mother of God, pray for us sinners, now and at the hour of our death. Amen.*

• *Glory be...*

2nd Day: Most mighty spirit, my angel guardian, I pray you, by that supreme felicity you enjoy in seeing God, obtain for me grace to walk always in the presence of God, so that I may always live a perfect Christian life.

• *Our Father...*
• *Hail Mary...*
• *Glory be...*

3rd Day: Most perfect executor of the will of God, my faithful guardian, I pray that you, by the vigilant and loving eagerness with which you guard me, obtain for me the grace of being always anxious to know and accomplish everything that God asks of me.

- *Our Father...*
- *Hail Mary...*
- *Glory be...*

4th Day: My most zealous protector and dear angel guardian, I pray, that you, by the charge which God has given you to guard me in all my ways as a mother carries in her arms her beloved child, avert from me all occasions of sin, and preserve me from all perils which could make me offend God, and repress the temptations of the infernal enemy and my own passions so that having conquered the enemies of my salvation, I may walk with ease, by the grace of God, in the way of his commandments, until I die.

- *Our Father...*
- *Hail Mary...*
- *Glory be...*

5th Day: Most faithful guide, my angel guardian, I pray you, by the mission God has confided to you to lead me on the road to Heaven, obtain for me grace to follow faithfully and constantly the light which you show me. Show me the evil I must avoid, the good I must do, and always encourage me to practice virtue until the last moment of my life.

- *Our Father...*
- *Hail Mary...*
- *Glory be...*

6th Day: Dearest friend, my good angel, I pray that you, by the great love you have for me, obtain for me the consolation of always praying in my troubles, so that I may obtain God's mercy always.

- *Our Father...*
- *Hail Mary...*
- *Glory be...*

7th Day: Most powerful intercessor, my faithful guardian, I pray that you, by the zeal God has given you for the eternal salvation of my soul, obtain for me the grace of having an

ardent and prudent zeal for the salvation of my neighbor.
  • *Hail Mary...*
  • *Glory be...*

8th Day: O most pure spirit, dear angel guardian, I pray that you, by the burning love you have for the Immaculate Virgin Mother of God, the Queen of Angels, to obtain for me great purity of soul and body, that at my death I may be found worthy to associate with you in Paradise.
  • *Our Father...*
  • *Hail Mary...*
  • *Glory be...*

9th Day: O sweetest angel, my faithful and loving guardian, how can I thank you sufficiently for the ardent love and faithful vigilance with which you have always watched, and will watch over me, until you have led me safely into the sweet presence of God. Pray for me that I may thank you by obedience to your holy inspirations, so that loving you daily more and more, I may merit to be with you for all eternity.
  • *Our Father...*
  • *Hail Mary...*
  • *Glory be...*

O you holy angels, our guardians, defend us in the day of battle that we may not be lost in the dreadful judgment.
  • *God hath given his angels charge concerning you.*
  • *To keep you in all your ways.*

Let Us Pray

O God, who in your unspeakable providence sent your angels to keep guard over us, grant that we may be continually defended by their protection, and rejoice eternally with them in Heaven. Through our Lord Jesus Christ. Amen.

"*The Guardian Angel," by Bernardo Strozzi (circa 1628).*
Courtesy Wikimedia Commons.

Litany of Our Holy Angel Guardian

Lord, have mercy.
Lord, have mercy.
Christ, have mercy.
Christ, have mercy.
Lord, have mercy.
Lord, have mercy.
Christ, hear us.
Christ, graciously hear us.
God the Father of Heaven, **have mercy on us.**

God the Son, Redeemer of the world, *have mercy on us.*
God the Holy Ghost, *have mercy on us.*
Holy Trinity, one God, *have mercy on us.*
Holy Mary, Queen of Angels, *pray for us.*
Holy Angel, my guardian, *pray for us.*
Holy Angel, my prince, *pray for us.*
Holy Angel, my monitor, *pray for us.*
Holy Angel, my counselor, *pray for us.*
Holy Angel, my defender, *pray for us.*
Holy Angel, my steward, *pray for us.*
Holy Angel, my friend, *pray for us.*
Holy Angel, my negotiator, *pray for us.*
Holy Angel, my intercessor, *pray for us.*
Holy Angel, my patron, *pray for us.*
Holy Angel, my director, *pray for us.*
Holy Angel, my ruler, *pray for us.*
Holy Angel, my protector, *pray for us.*
Holy Angel, my comforter, *pray for us.*
Holy Angel, my brother, *pray for us.*
Holy Angel, my teacher, *pray for us.*
Holy Angel, my shepherd, *pray for us.*
Holy Angel, my witness, *pray for us.*
Holy Angel, my helper, *pray for us.*
Holy Angel, my watcher, *pray for us.*
Holy Angel, my conductor, *pray for us.*
Holy Angel, my preserver, *pray for us.*
Holy Angel, my instructor, *pray for us.*
Holy Angel, my enlightener, *pray for us.*
Lamb of God, who takes away the sins of the world. *Spare us, O Lord.*
Lamb of God, who takes away the sins of the world. *Graciously hear us, O Lord.*
Lamb of God, who takes away the sins of the world.

"The Guardian Angel," by Bartolomeo Cavarozzi (1590-1625).
Courtesy Wikimedia Commons.

Have mercy on us.
Christ, hear us.
Christ, graciously hear us.
Pray for us, O holy Angel Guardian, that we may be made worthy of the promises of Christ.

Let Us Pray

Almighty, everlasting God, who, in the counsel of your ineffable goodness, has appointed to all the faithful, from their mother's womb, a special Angel Guardian of their body and soul; grant that I may so love and honor the angel whom you have so mercifully given me, that, protected by the bounty of your grace, I may merit to behold, with my angel and all the angelic host, the glory of your countenance in the heavenly country. Who lives and reigns, world without end. Amen.

"An Angel," by unknown (circa 1400s). Courtesy Wikimedia Commons.

Byzantine Prayer to the Guardian Angel
(Catholic prayer by Peter the Studite)

O Guardian Angel, protector of my soul and body, to your care I have been entrusted by Christ. Obtain for me the forgiveness of the sins I have committed today. Protect me from the snares of my enemy, that I may never again offend God by sin. Pray for me, your sinful and unworthy servant that, through your help, I may become worthy of the grace and mercy of the most Holy Trinity and of the immaculate Mother of our Lord God, Jesus Christ. Amen.

CHAPTER 4: ALL HOLY ANGELS

"The Shepherds and the Christmas Angel" by Carl Bloch (1879). Courtesy Wikimedia Commons.

In 1916, an angel visited Lucia dos Santos and her cousins Francisco and Jacinta Marto in Portugal while the children tended sheep and played. In the first appearance, a strong wind shook the olive trees before a figure of a youth, about 15 years old, descended. He was "whiter than snow, which the sun rendered transparent as if it were of crystal, and of great beauty. We were surprised and half absorbed. We did not say a word. While coming closer to us, the Angel said: 'Do not fear! I am the Angel of Peace. Pray with me.'

And kneeling on the earth, he bent his forehead to the ground. Prompted by a supernatural movement, we imitated him and repeated the words which we heard him pronounce: 'My God, I believe in Thee, I adore Thee, I hope in Thee and I love Thee. I ask pardon for all those who do not believe in

Thee, do not adore Thee, do not hope in Thee and do not love Thee.'" The angel, who later revealed himself as the Guardian Angel of Portugal, prepared the children for visions of Our Lady of Fatima.

"Angel of the Annunciation" by Titan (circa 1520). Courtesy Wikimedia Commons.

PRAYERS TAUGHT BY THE ANGEL IN FATIMA

Pardon Prayer

My God, I believe in you, I adore you, I hope in you, and I love you. I ask pardon for those who do not believe in you, do not adore you, do not hope in you, and do not love you. Amen.

Eucharistic Prayer

Most Holy Trinity, I adore You! My God, my God, I love You in the Most Blessed Sacrament. Amen.

The Angel's Prayer

O most Holy Trinity, Father, Son and Holy Spirit, I adore you profoundly, and I offer you the Most Precious Body, Blood, Soul and Divinity of Jesus Christ, present in all the tabernacles of the world, in reparation for the outrages, sacrileges and indifference by which he is offended. And by the infinite merits of his most Sacred Heart and the Immaculate Heart of Mary, I beg the conversion of poor sinners. Amen.

"St. Cecilia and the Angels" by Paul Delaroche (1836). Courtesy Wikimedia Commons.

Short Prayer to the Angels

Angels and Archangels, Thrones and Dominations, Principalities and Powers, Virtues of the heavens, Cherubim and Seraphim, praise the Lord forever. Praise the Lord, all you his angels, who are mighty in strength and who carry out his commands. Praise the Lord, all you his Hosts, his servants who do his will. Holy Angel who strengthened Jesus Christ our Lord, come and strengthen us also. Come and do not delay. Amen.

"Angels Dancing" by Giovanni di Paolo (circa 1436). Courtesy Wikimedia Commons.

Act of Consecration to the Nine Choirs of Angels
(1600s French prayer)

Blessed spirits of the heavenly court, invincible defenders of the interests of God, we ask your help in the coming of the reign of the most adorable Jesus so that all people making profession of one faith may conduct themselves according to the purity of its maxims, lead lives conformable to its rules, and that the sacred interests of God alone may be maintained in all hearts.

We ask this of the Father of all mercies, by your powerful intercession, O princes of the heavenly army, so that the empire of sin and the devils may be destroyed, so the Gospel may be preached to all nations, so the holy name of God may be adored and glorified, and so all hearts may praise God and be in perfect submission to his holy will.

Come then, Angels and Archangels, hasten to establish everywhere the reign of God.

Holy Principalities, govern all hearts and subject them to the empire of Jesus and Mary.

"Three Guardian Angels" by Franz Kadlik (1822). Courtesy Wikimedia Commons.

Admirable Powers, confound the demons and ruin the designs of hell and the plans of all the enemies of God.

Divine Virtues, make souls walk in the solid road of divine love.

Glorious Dominations, show everyone God's holy will towards them.

Sweet Thrones, establish firmly in our hearts the peace that our Lord has left us.

Cherubim, doctors of the science of saints, communicate its sweet light to earth.

And you, Seraphim, princes of pure love, grant that people live only in love's flames so that God alone may be glorified forever and ever. Amen.

Another Consecration to the Holy Angels

Holy Angels, I implore you to assist me. Help me to adore God and the Most Holy Sacrament of the Altar to contemplate the word and works of God's salvation, to imitate Christ and the love of his cross in a spirit of expiation, to fulfill my mission within the Church, and to serve humbly after the example of Mary, my heavenly Mother, your Queen.

"The Passage of a Soul" by Louis Janmot (1854). Courtesy Wikimedia Commons.

My good Guardian Angel, who continually beholds the face of our Father in Heaven, God entrusted me to you from the very beginning of my life. I thank you with all my heart for your loving care. I commit myself to you and promise you my love and fidelity. I beg you to protect me against my own weakness and against the attacks of the wicked spirits; enlighten my mind and my heart so I may always know and accomplish the will of God; and lead me to union with God the Father, the Son, and the Holy Spirit. Amen.

A Prayer to All Angels
(1600s French prayer)

O angels, so pure and holy, truly happy spirits, who bow before God and contemplate so joyfully the countenance of the heavenly Solomon, who has communicated to you the most enlightened wisdom, who ennobled you with so many privileges, and made you worthy of such eminent glory.

*"The Dream of St. Joseph" by Anton Raphael Meng (circa 1773).
Courtesy Wikimedia Commons.*

You who are such brilliant stars that you appear with splendor in the highest Heaven, I ask you to spread your happy influence over my soul, preserve my faith in its purity, my hope in its firmness, my heart in its integrity, and grant that I may always advance in the love of God and my neighbor.

I pray to you also, O blessed angels, that you will conduct me, by your celestial power, in the way of humility, of which you have ever shown me an example, so that after this life I may deserve to contemplate with you the supreme beauty of our heavenly Father, and be received in the place of one of those stars who, by their pride, fell from Heaven. Amen.

"Two Angels with the Emblems of Justice" by unknown (circa 1500s). Courtesy Wikimedia Commons.

Prayer to the Holy Angel Guardians of all People & Places

(1700s English prayer)

O Holy Angel, who was appointed by the Divine Goodness to be my guardian, to conduct my blindness, teach my ignorance, strengthen my weakness, and energize my laziness; I heartily praise our common Lord for so great a benefit; and thank you for the many good works you have done for me, defending me amid so many dangers both spiritual and corporal; but especially by withholding me from sin, and preserving me when I was hastening to my own destruction.

I humbly ask you to continue the same care on my behalf, until you have brought my soul to the happy port of everlasting salvation. All you good Angels (guardians of all people, cities, provinces, and countries), I humbly offer you my prayers to perform all your charitable works towards me, towards this city and country, towards all my relatives, friends, benefactors, neighbors and acquaintances.

Direct our thoughts, words and deeds towards the salvation of our souls so that by keeping the Commandments of God, we may, by his grace, be made worthy to live with you in eternal joy. Through Jesus Christ our Lord and only Savior. Amen.

"An Angel Comforts Jesus in the Garden of Gethsemane" by Carl Heinrich Bloch (1865-1879). Courtesy Wikimedia Commons.

Prayer to the Angel who Strengthened Our Lord in His Agony

O Holy Angel who strengthened Jesus Christ our Lord, come and strengthen us also; come and delay not. I salute you, Holy Angel who comforted my Jesus in his agony, and with you I praise the most Holy Trinity for having chosen you from among all the Holy Angels to comfort and strengthen him who is the comfort and strength of all who are suffering.

By the honor you enjoyed and by the obedience, humility and love with which you assisted the sacred humanity of Jesus, my Savior, when he was fainting with sorrow at seeing the sins of the world and especially my sins, I ask you to obtain for me perfect sorrow for my sins; strengthen me in the afflictions that now overwhelm me, and in all other trials that I will be exposed to from today onwards, and, in particular, when I find myself in my final agony. Amen.

Rosary of the Holy Angels

On the Cross, pray the *Creed,* then the *Our Father*, and the *Hail Mary.*

• *I believe in God, the Father Almighty, creator of Heaven and earth; and in Jesus Christ, his only son, our lord: who was conceived by the Holy Spirit, born of the Virgin Mary; suffered under Pontius Pilate, was crucified, died and was buried. He descended into hell; the third day he rose again from the dead; he ascended into Heaven, is seated at the right hand of God the Father Almighty; from thence he shall come to judge the living and the dead. I believe in the Holy Spirit, the Holy Catholic Church, the communion of saints, the forgiveness of sins, the resurrection of the body, and life everlasting. Amen.*

• **Our Father, who art in Heaven, hallowed be thy Name, thy kingdom come, thy will be done, on earth as it is in Heaven. Give us this day our daily bread, and forgive us our trespasses, as we forgive those who trespass against us. And lead us not into temptation, but deliver us from evil. Amen.**

"*An Angel and the Three Marys at the Tomb of Jesus*" *by Bartolomeo Schedoni (1613). Courtesy Wikimedia Commons.*

• Hail Mary, full of grace, the Lord is with thee: blessed art thou amongst women, and blessed is the fruit of thy womb, Jesus. Holy Mary, mother of God, pray for us sinners, now and at the hour of our death. Amen.

On the large beads, the *Glory Be* or the *Hail Mary*.

• Glory be to the Father and to the Son and to the Holy Spirit. As it was in the beginning is now, and ever shall be, world without end. Amen.

If this Rosary is offered in honor of your Guardian Angel, say the "*Angele Dei*."

• Angel of God, my guardian dear, to whom his love commits me here; ever this (day, night) be at my side, to light and guard, to rule and guide. Amen.

Or you may say: "*My good angel, I love, and will love you.*"

If this Rosary is offered in honor of the Nine Choirs of Angels, you can substitute: "*Holy angels, I love, and will love you.*"

"The Resurrection of Christ" by Carl H. Bloch (1875). Courtesy Wikimedia Commons.

Chaplet of the Holy Angels

O my Jesus, I offer this chaplet to your Divine Heart, that you may render it perfect, thus giving joy to your Holy Angels, and so they may keep me under their holy protection, above all at the hour of my death to which I invite them with all my heart. Strengthened by their presence, I will await death with joy and be preserved from the assaults of hell.

I ask you also, dear Angels, to visit immediately the souls in Purgatory, especially my parents, my friends, my benefactors; help them so that they will soon be delivered. Do not forget me either after my death.

This I beg you with all my heart, through the Sacred Heart of Jesus and the Immaculate Heart of Mary.

St. Michael, I recommend the hour of my death to you. Hold the Evil One prisoner, so that he may not battle against me or harm my soul.

St. Gabriel, obtain for me from God lively faith, strong hope, ardent charity and great devotion to the Blessed Sacrament of the Altar.

St. Raphael, lead me constantly on the road of virtue and perfection.

My Holy Guardian Angel, obtain for me divine inspiration and the special grace to be faithful.

1) O ardent Seraphim, obtain for me a burning love for God.

Our Father...

Three Hail Marys...

2) O Cherubim brilliant with light, obtain for me true knowledge of the science of the saints.

Our Father...

Three Hail Marys...

3) O admirable Thrones, obtain for me peace and tranquility of heart.

Our Father...

Three Hail Marys...

4) O exalted Dominions, obtain for me victory over all evil thoughts.

Our Father...

Three Hail Marys...

5) O invincible Powers, obtain for me strength against all evil spirits.

Our Father...

Three Hail Marys...

6) O most serene Virtues, obtain for me obedience and perfect justice.

Our Father...

Three Hail Marys...

7) O Principalities, who accomplish wonders, obtain for me plenitude of all virtues and perfection.

"Jacob Wrestling with the Angel" by Alexander Louis Leloir (1865). Courtesy Wikimedia Commons.

Our Father...

Three Hail Marys...

8) O holy Archangels, obtain for me conformity to the will of God.

Our Father...

Three Hail Marys...

9) O holy Angels, O faithful Guardian Angels, obtain for me true humility and great confidence in the divine mercy.

Our Father...

Three Hail Marys...

Prayer in Honor of All Angels

I honor and reverence you, O Glorious St. Michael, chief of all the Angels.

I honor and reverence you, O Blessed St. Gabriel for delivering that happy message to the Blessed Virgin Mary.

I honor and reverence you, O St. Raphael, for rendering to the young Tobias so clear a testimony of God's ineffable goodness to man.

"Angel Musicians" by Hans Memling (circa 1480). Courtesy Wikimedia Commons.

I honor and reverence you, O most ardent Seraphim, who burn continually in the flames of the love of God.

I honor and reverence you, O most holy Cherubim, who surpass all other Angels in the clear knowledge of God.

I honor and reverence you, O most happy Thrones, in whom the eternal Majesty does repose, and who dispose our souls to peace and tranquility.

I honor and reverence you, O most noble Dominations, who by the great authority bestowed on you by God, rule all other spirits of inferior rank.

I honor and reverence you, O most powerful Virtues, who are appointed by the sovereign King of Heaven to the regency and governing of all the soldiers in Heaven.

I honor and reverence you, O most valiant Powers, who by your might repress the insolence of the powers of hell and oppose all the continuous malicious plots against us.

I honor and reverence you, O invincible Archangels, to whom is given the protection and care of people and countries, and who reveal the most sublime mysteries to them for their welfare.

I honor and reverence you also, O most humble Angels, who disdain not to communicate with men, and undertake their patronage and protection. Amen.

"Christ Surrounded by Musician Angels" by Hans Memling (circa 1480). Courtesy Wikimedia Commons.

Litany of the Holy Angels
(from the 1800s)

Lord, have mercy.
Lord, have mercy.
Christ, have mercy.
Christ, have mercy.
Lord, have mercy.
Lord, have mercy.
Christ, hear us.
Christ, graciously hear us.
God the Father of Heaven, *have mercy on us.*
God the Son, Redeemer of the world, *have mercy on us.*
God the Holy Ghost, *have mercy on us.*
Holy Trinity, one God, *have mercy on us.*
Holy Mary, Queen of Angels, *pray for us.*
Holy Mother of God, *pray for us.*
Holy Virgin of virgins, *pray for us.*
St. Michael, defender of the people of God, *pray for us.*

St. Michael, who drove from Heaven Lucifer and his rebel crew, *pray for us.*

St. Michael, who cast down to hell the accuser of our brethren, *pray for us.*

St. Gabriel, who expounded to Daniel the heavenly vision, *pray for us.*

St. Gabriel, who foretold to Zachary the birth and ministry of John the Baptist, *pray for us.*

St. Gabriel, who announced to Mary the Incarnation of the Divine Word, *pray for us.*

St. Raphael, who led Tobias safe through his journey to his home again, *pray for us.*

St. Raphael, who delivered Sara from the devil, *pray for us.*

St. Raphael, who restored sight to Tobias the elder, *pray for us.*

All you holy Angels, who stand upon the high and lofty throne of God, *pray for us.*

Who cry to him continually, *"Holy, holy, holy"*, *pray for us.*

Who dispel the darkness of our minds and give us light, *pray for us.*

Who are messengers of heavenly things to men, *pray for us.*

Who have been appointed by God to be our guardians, *pray for us.*

Who always behold the face of our Father in Heaven, *pray for us.*

Who rejoice over one sinner doing penance, *pray for us.*

Who struck the Sodomites with blindness, *pray for us.*

Who led Lot out of the midst of the ungodly, *pray for us.*

Who ascended and descended the ladder of Jacob, *pray for us.*

Who delivered the divine law to Moses on Mount Sinai, *pray for us.*

Who brought good tidings when Christ was born, *pray for us.*

"Angel of Death" by Émile Jean-Horace Vernet (1851). Courtesy Wikimedia Commons.

Who ministered to him in the desert, *pray for us.*

Who comforted him in his agony, *pray for us.*

Who sat in white garments at his sepulcher, *pray for us.*

Who appeared to the disciples as he went up into Heaven, *pray for us.*

Who shall go before him bearing the standard of the cross when he comes to judgment, *pray for us.*

Who shall gather together the elect at the end of the world, *pray for us.*

Who shall separate the wicked from the just, *pray for us.*

Who offer to God the prayers of those who pray, *pray for us.*

Who assist us at the hour of death, *pray for us.*

Who carried Lazarus into Abraham's bosom, *pray for us.* Who conduct to Heaven the purified souls of the just, *pray for us.*

Who perform signs and wonders by the power of God, *pray for us.*

Who are sent to minister to those who shall receive the inheritance of salvation, *pray for us.*

Who would cure Babylon, and when she will not be cured, depart and forsake her, *pray for us.*

Who are set over kingdoms and provinces, *pray for us.*

Who have often put to flight armies of enemies, *pray for us.*

Who have often delivered God's servants from prison and other perils of this life, *pray for us.*

Who have often consoled the holy martyrs in their torments, *pray for us.*

Who take special care of the prelates and leaders of the Church and all who are under their charge, *pray for us.*

All you holy orders of blessed Spirits, *pray for us.*

From all dangers, deliver us, O Lord, by your holy Angels.

From the snares of the devil, *deliver us, O Lord.*

From all heresy and schism, *deliver us, O Lord.*

From plague, famine, and war, *deliver us, O Lord.*

From sudden and unexpected death, *deliver us, O Lord.*

From everlasting death in Hell, *deliver us, O Lord.*

We sinners, *we ask you to hear us.*

Through your holy Angels, *we ask you to hear us.*

That you spare us, *we ask you to hear us.*

That you pardon us, *we ask you to hear us.*

That you govern and preserve your holy Church, *we ask you to hear us.*

That you protect our Apostolic Pope and all ecclesiastical orders, *we ask you to hear us.*

That you grant peace and security to kings and all Christian leaders, *we ask you to hear us.*

That you give and preserve the fruits of the earth, *we ask you to hear us.*

That you grant eternal rest to all the faithful departed, *we ask you to hear us.*

Lamb of God, who takes away the sins of the world, *spare us, O Lord.*

Lamb of God, who takes away the sins of the world,

"Release of St. Peter" by Bernardo Strozzi (1635). Courtesy Wikimedia Commons.

Graciously hear us, O Lord.
Lamb of God, who takes away the sins of the world,
Have mercy on us.
Lord, have mercy.
Christ, have mercy.
Lord, have mercy.

   • *Our Father, who art in Heaven, hallowed be thy Name, thy kingdom come, thy will be done, on earth as it is in Heaven. Give us this day our daily bread, and forgive us our trespasses, as we forgive those who trespass against us. And lead us not into temptation, but deliver us from evil. Amen.*

Let Us Pray

O God, who dispenses the services of angels and men in a wonderful order, mercifully grant that our life may be protected on earth by those who always do you service in Heaven. Through Jesus Christ our Lord. Amen.

"Abraham and the Three Angels" by Giovanni Battista Tiepolo (1770).
Courtesy Wikimedia Commons.

Another Litany of the Holy Angels

O God, the Father of Heaven, *have mercy on us.*

O God, the Son, Redeemer of the world, *have mercy on us.*

O God, the Holy Ghost, proceeding from the Father and the Son, *have mercy on us.*

Holy Mary, Mother of God and Queen of Angels, *pray for us.*

Holy Angels, who, standing before the high and mighty throne of God, sing continually, *"Holy, holy, holy," pray for us.*

Holy Angels, who always behold the face of God in Heaven, serve before his throne, obey his word, and do his will, *pray for us.*

Holy Angels, who are committed by God to the care and

custody of man, *pray for us.*

Holy Angels, governors of provinces, protectors of kingdoms and nations, defenders of the church, conservators of the elect, *pray for us.*

Holy Angels, carrying up the prayers and services of men to God, and bringing down God's blessing unto men, *pray for us.*

Holy Angels, who excel in strength, restraining the powers of evil spirits and the malice of wicked men, *pray for us.*

Holy Angels, who rejoice in the conversion of any one sinner who does penance, *pray for us.*

St. Michael, prince of the heavenly host, who cast the dragon with his apostate angels out of Heaven; mighty Prince who always stands to help the people of God, *pray for us.*

St. Michael, the receiver of the souls of the faithful, and who conducts them into Paradise, *pray for us.*

St. Gabriel, who revealed to Daniel the sacred visions, who warred against the prince of the Persians for the people of God; who announced to Zachary the birth and office of St. John the Baptist; and, sent from God to the Blessed Virgin, was the happy messenger of the Incarnation of the eternal Word of God, *pray for us.*

St. Raphael, one of the seven who assist before our Lord, the holy conductor of Tobias, the restorer of sight, and powerful expeller of evil spirits, *pray for us.*

Holy Seraphim, who with a burning coal purified the lips of Isaiah, *pray for us.*

Holy Cherubim, who keep the way of the Tree of Life, *pray for us.*

O Holy Angels, who, in executing judgment on Sodom, delivered Lot, *pray for us.*

Holy Angels, who ascended and descended on Jacob's ladder, *pray for us.*

Holy Angels, who delivered Jacob from all evil, *pray for us.*

O Prince of the Host of God, who was sent to aid Joshua and who destroyed the Assyrians, warring against God's people, a hundred four-score and five thousand in one night, *pray for us.*

Holy Angel, who, when Daniel was cast into the lion's den, shut the lions' mouths so they might not hurt him, *pray for us.*

Holy Angels, who joyfully sung, *"Glory to God on high, at the birth of the savior of mankind," **pray for us.***

Holy Angels, who ministered to our Lord as he hungered in the wilderness, *pray for us.*

Holy Angel, who comforted our Lord in his agony, *pray for us.*

Holy Angels, who first declared the joyful news of our Lord's Resurrection, *pray for us.*

O you Angels of God, who brought out of prison and set at liberty the apostles, and St. Peter, and struck proud Herod with an ignominious death, *pray for us.*

Holy Angels, who carried the soul of Lazarus into Abraham's bosom, *pray for us.*

O Holy Angels, who shall come with our savior in his majesty to judgment, and at the end of the world shall gather the elect from the four winds, and separate the wicked from among the just, and gather all scandals out of the Kingdom of Christ, *pray for us.*

O all you Orders of blessed spirits, Angels, and Archangels, Virtues and Thrones, Dominions, Principalities, Powers, Cherubim, and Seraphim, *pray for us.*

O Christ, who is placed above all Principalities, and Powers, and Thrones, and Dominions, and every name that is named, not only in this world but the world to come, ***have mercy on us.***

From all dangers, ***by your Holy Angels deliver us O Lord.***

From the temptations, snares, and illusions of the devil, by your Holy Angels, deliver us O Lord.

"Hagar and the Angel" by Pieter Lastman (1614). Courtesy Wikimedia Commons.

From all filthy and unclean thoughts and suggestions, *by your Holy Angels deliver us O Lord.*

From the advice and malice of wicked people, and all evil company,*by your Holy Angels deliver us O Lord.*

From sudden and unexpected death, *by your Holy Angels deliver us O Lord.*

We sinners, *we ask you to hear us.*

That you would spare us and give your Holy Angels to care for us and keep us in all our ways, *we ask you to hear us.*

That you would direct and govern your Church, and grant to all societies unity, peace, and harmony by the ministration of your Angels, *we ask you to hear us.*

That you will at the hour of death guard us with the defense and protection of your Holy Angels, *we ask you to hear us.*

That you will transport our souls, when they depart from our bodies, into the heavenly mansions, by the ministry of your Holy Angels, *we ask you to hear us.*

That you will grant eternal rest to all the faithful departed in the blessed company of your Holy Angels, *we ask you to hear us.*

Lamb of God, you take away the sins of the world, *have mercy on us.*

Lamb of God, you take away the sins of the world, *grant us peace.*

• *Our Father, who art in Heaven, hallowed be thy Name, thy kingdom come, thy will be done, on earth as it is in Heaven. Give us this day our daily bread, and forgive us our trespasses, as we forgive those who trespass against us. And lead us not into temptation, but deliver us from evil. Amen.*

• *Glory be to the Father and to the Son and to the Holy Spirit. As it was in the beginning is now, and ever shall be, world without end. Amen.*

Before the angels I will sing praise to you. I will adore your holy Temple, and praise your name, O Lord. O Lord, hear our prayers. And let our cry come to you.

Let Us Pray

O eternal God, who in your wonderful providence made the angels ministering spirits and sent them on missions for the good of your elect, behold with pity the temptations and dangers to which the frailty of our nature is perpetually exposed, and give your holy angels charge to bear us in their hands, and cover us under the shadow of their wings, that, being guided through the desert of this life by their safe conduct, we may enter at last into the land of Promise, and rejoice for ever in their blessed society. Through Jesus Christ our Lord.

O Almighty and everlasting God, who made us after your own image and appointed your holy angels for our keepers, grant to your servants, that by their defense and care we happily pass through all dangers of body and soul, and attain to everlasting joys, together with them and you. Through Jesus Christ our Lord.

Angel with an Olive Branch" by Hans Memling (circa 1433-1494). Courtesy Wikimedia Commons.

We ask you, O Angelical Spirit, our faithful guardian and keeper, direct and guide us this day and forever in the way of peace, prosperity and safety.

Defend us from every evil spirit and dangerous temptation until we arrive at the blessed vision in our heavenly country; and there, together with you and all the saints, praise the Savior of us all forever and ever. Amen.

"The Flight of Lot and His Family from Sodom" by Peter Paul Rubens (circa 1615). Courtesy Wikimedia Commons.

Litany to the Nine Choirs of Angels

Lord, have mercy on us.
Christ, have mercy on us.
Lord, have mercy on us.
Christ, hear us.
Christ, graciously hear us.
God the Father of Heaven, ***have mercy on us.***
God the Son, Redeemer of the world, ***have mercy on us.***
God the Holy Ghost, ***have mercy on us.***
Holy Trinity, one God, ***have mercy on us.***
Holy Mary, Queen of angels, ***pray for us.***
St. Michael, who always was the defender of the people of God, ***pray for us.***
St. Gabriel, who was appointed to announce the incarnation of the Eternal Word, ***pray for us.***

"St. Raymond Nonnatus being fed by Angels" by a follower of Eugenio Cajes (1630). Courtesy Wikimedia Commons.

St. Raphael, the conductor of Tobias, *pray for us.*

Holy Seraphim, *pray for us.*

Holy Cherubim, *pray for us.*

Holy Thrones, *pray for us.*

Holy Dominations, *pray for us.*

Holy Virtues, *pray for us.*

Holy Powers, *pray for us.*

Holy Principalities, *pray for us.*

Holy Archangels, *pray for us.*

Holy Angels, *pray for us.*

O you, who stand around the throne of the most high God, *pray for us.*

O you, who always see the face of the heavenly Father, *pray for us.*

O you, who God has committed to the care and guardianship of mankind, *pray for us.*

O you, who brought Lot and his family from the midst of the wicked, *pray for us.*

O you, who ministered to Christ in the desert when he put the tempter to flight, *pray for us.*

O you, who carried Lazarus into Abraham's bosom, *pray for us.*

"St. Maurice & an Angel" by Bernardo Strozzi (1640). Courtesy Wikimedia Commons.

O you, who often delivered the servants of God from prison and dangers, *pray for us.*

O you, who often comforted the holy martyrs in the midst of torments, *pray for us.*

O you, who carry up and offer to God the prayers of his servants, *pray for us.*

O you, who have joy in Heaven upon one sinner's doing penance, *pray for us.*

O you, who have been set over nations, kingdoms, and provinces, *pray for us.*

O you, who will attend upon Jesus Christ when he comes to judge the world, *pray for us.*

O you ministering spirits, sent to minister for those who shall receive the inheritance of salvation, *pray for us.*

O you angels of the Lord, who are mighty in strength and execute his word, hearkening to the voice of his orders, *pray for us.*

O you, the hosts of the Lord, his ministers, who do his will, *pray for us.*

O you holy angel, my faithful guardian, *pray for us.*

Holy angel, my guide and my friend, *pray for us.*

Holy angel, my counselor and powerful intercessor, *pray for us.*

Holy angel, my protector and comforter, *pray for us.*

All you orders of blessed spirits, *pray for us.*

Be merciful to us, *spare us, O Lord.*

Be merciful to us, *hear us, O Lord.*

From all dangers, by your holy angels, *O Lord, deliver us.*

From the snares of the devil, by your holy angels, *O Lord, deliver us.*

From all sin, by your holy angels, *O Lord, deliver us.*

From a sudden and unprovided death, by your holy angels, *O Lord, deliver us.*

We sinners ask you to hear us.

Through the intercession of your holy angels, *we ask you to hear us.*

That you spare us, *we ask you to hear us.*

That you pardon us, *we ask you to hear us.*

That you preserve and govern your holy Church, *we ask you to hear us.*

That you grant peace and unity to all people, *we ask you to hear us.*

That you give eternal rest to all the faithful departed, *we ask you to hear us.*

That you send your holy Angels to us at the hour of our death, *we ask you to hear us.*

That you, after our death, receive our souls, through the hands of the Angels, into eternal bliss, *we ask you to hear us.*

Son of God, you take away the sins of the world, *have mercy on us.*

Lamb of God, you take away the sins of the word, *grant us peace.*

O you holy orders of blessed Spirits, *pray for us.*

That we may be made worthy of the promises of Christ.

"The Vocation of St. Aloysius Gonzaga" by Guercino (circa 1650). Courtesy Wikimedia Commons.

Let Us Pray

O God, who, in your wonderful providence, has been pleased to appoint your Holy Angels for our guardians, mercifully hear our prayers, and grant we may rest safely under their protection, and enjoy their fellowship forever, through Jesus Christ our Lord. Amen.

*"Holy Communion Surrounded by a Garland" by Jan Davidszoon de Heem
(1648). Courtesy Wikimedia Commons.*

To the Angels & Saints after Communion

Holy angels and elect of God, praise the Lord our God. Bless his holy name. Great and marvelous are the things that he has done for love of me. Jesus is mine; he has come to visit me.

Holy angel guardian, and you, my patron saint, what joy must now be yours! The God whom you worship is now within my heart. Give thanks to him for me, give thanks to God my savior, for you can praise him far more worthily than I can. Pray for me also that I may never again by sin banish my Jesus from my heart. Now I will be happy, since Jesus my savior is within my heart. Let nothing separate me from him.

Pray for me, saints of God; ask for me grace to remain continually in your blessed company, and one day to see our Lord, no longer under the veils of the Eucharist, but face to face in the glory of Heaven, there to praise and adore him throughout a happy eternity. Amen.

A Prayer to the Saints and Angels

All you holy saints of God, particularly you whose name I bear, and all you holy angels of God, especially you whom God has appointed to be my guardian, intercede for me and defend me from all danger. Amen.

To All Angels and Saints

Angels, Archangels, Thrones and Dominations, Principalities and Powers, and Virtues of Heaven, Cherubim and Seraphim, patriarchs and prophets, holy doctors of the law, apostles, all martyrs of Christ, holy confessors, virgins of the Lord, anchorites, and all saints, intercede for us.

• *All ye holy men and women, saints of God. Intercede for us.*

Let Us Pray

Almighty and everlasting God, who willed that we should profit by the merits of all your saints, we ask that you bestow on us abundant mercy which we desire. Through Christ our Lord. Amen.

"The Last Judgment Polyptych" by Rogier van der Weyden (circa 1446). Courtesy Wikimedia Commons.

Litany of the Saints and Angels

(1700s English prayer)

Lord have mercy on us,

Christ have mercy on us,

Lord have mercy on us,

God the Father, creator of the world, *have mercy on us.*

O God the Son, redeemer of mankind, *have mercy on us.*

O God the Holy Ghost, perfecter of the elect, *have mercy on us.*

O Sacred Trinity, three Persons and one God, *have mercy on us.*

O Blessed Virgin Mother of our Lord Jesus Christ, *pray for us.* That we may adore the mystery of our Savior's Incarnation and freely offer ourselves to him, who freely gave himself for us.

"The Resurrection of the Dead" by Victor Mottez (1870). Courtesy Wikimedia Commons.

O Blessed Virgin, most glorious Queen of Saints and Angels, *pray for us.* That we may praise the bounty of our Lord, who has so highly exalted the humility of his handmaid, raising your immaculate body from the grave to crown you in Heaven with glory and honor.

O Blessed Virgin, most gracious protectress of the servants of your son, *pray for us.* That by the merits of his passion our sins may be pardoned, and by his acceptance of your intercession we may be delivered from all dangers.

Blessed Angels, who in the heavenly choirs perpetually sing praise to God, *pray for us.* That the great and holy name of our creator may be sanctified by us on earth, as it is by you in Heaven.

Blessed Angels, whose charity is great and who rejoice at the conversion of a sinner, *pray for us.* That we may diligently improve the good you see in us and sincerely repent of and amend the great evils we know to be in ourselves.

Blessed Angels, who continually behold the face of God and are ready to dispense his benefits to us, *pray for us.* That living in the fear of God we may enjoy your care and after our death we will be led by you into Paradise.

Blessed Patriarchs, who in times when grace was not so liberally given, nor the light of divine revelation so great, safely arrived to the state of glory, *pray for us.* That we may faithfully observe the law of God written in our hearts and not abuse the abundant grace of the Gospel by neglecting to do good deeds.

Blessed Prophets, who by divine inspiration, predicted the coming of the Messiah and, after a patient expectation of deliverance, were led by him with triumph into Heaven, *pray for us.* That we may admire the goodness of our Savior in his humble coming to redeem us, and prepare to account for our life at the time of his glorious appearance to judge us.

Blessed Apostles, who in this barren earth planted the Christian faith and watered it with your blood, *pray for us.* That we may constantly profess the ancient faith of the Catholic Church and practice the perfect charity of the early Christians.

Blessed Disciples of our Lord, who had the privilege to talk familiarly with Jesus, hearing his heavenly doctrine from himself and seeing his glorious miracles with your own eyes, *pray for us.* That we may always behave ourselves as if in the presence of our Redeemer, carefully striving to fulfill his holy laws, while thankfully acknowledging the wonders of his infinite power.

Blessed Martyrs, who, laying down a short and frail life, have secured a place for yourselves in eternity, *pray for us.* That we never offend God for fear of man, nor lose our souls to gain the world.

Blessed Confessors, who by the improvement of the talents entrusted to you, have entered into your master's joy, *pray for us.* That we may profitably use the gifts of grace and nature, which God has given us, to advance his glory, and obtain our own eternal joy.

"The Ecstasy of St. Rosalia of Palermo" by Theodoor Boeyermans (circa 1600s). Courtesy Wikimedia Commons.

Blessed Virgins, who imitating here on earth the purity of Angels, are forever espoused to the heavenly bridegroom, *pray for us.* That mortifying all sensual and inordinate desires, we may raise our affections to the glorious life of Heaven and there eternally settle our hearts on the chaste love of our Savior.

All you Holy Saints of Paradise, who, by the blissful vision of God, are secure of your own happiness, and, by your perfect charity are concerned for ours, *pray for us.* That the honor we give to your memories may affect our minds with a devotion to your virtues and we imitate your holy lives to bring us into the fellowship of your everlasting glory, through Jesus Christ our Lord.

And now, O sovereign Lord and merciful Redeemer, having implored the intercession of the Blessed Virgin Mother as well as all the holy Angels and glorious Saints, under the favor of their assistance, we appear before the throne of your majesty, and, relying on your own infinite goodness, humbly address our prayers to you.

Jesus, eternal son of the living God, *have mercy on us.*

Jesus, most blessed son of the Virgin Mary, *have mercy on us.*

Jesus, God and man, two natures yet but one Christ, *have mercy on us.*

Jesus, the glory of Heaven and joy of Angels, *have mercy on us.*

Jesus, king of Patriarchs, and light of the Prophets, *have mercy on us.*

Jesus, master of the Apostles and fortitude of the Martyrs, *have mercy on us.*

Jesus, the sanctity of Confessors and the purity of Virgins, *have mercy on us.*

Jesus, the crown of all the Saints in Heaven, and the only hope of your servants on earth, *have mercy on us.*

O Lamb of God, who takes away the sins of the world, *spare us O Jesus.*

O Lamb of God, who takes away the sins of the world, *hear us O Jesus.*

O Lamb of God, who takes away the sins of the world, *have mercy on us.*

Let Us Pray

Almighty God, and most merciful Father, who gave your only begotten son to be born of a humble Virgin, favorably receive the prayers of your servants which we here present to you, by the intercession of the Blessed Virgin Mary; and grant, that as her purity is exalted by you to the highest degree of glory among creatures, her charity may obtain for us the special assistance of your grace, through Jesus Christ, our Lord and only Savior.

"The Dream of St. Bruno" by Eustache Le Sueur (1645). Courtesy Wikimedia Commons.

O Eternal God, who in your wonderful providence made the Angels ministering spirits, and who sends them with messages for the good of your people; look with pity at the temptations and dangers our frail nature is always exposed to, and entrust your holy Angels to hold us in their hands and cover us under the shadow of their wings; that being guided through the desert of this life by their safe conduct, we may enter at last into the land of promise and rejoice forever in their blessed company. Through Jesus Christ our Lord and only Savior.

Most gracious God, author of all sanctity and lover of unity, whose wisdom has established an admirable communion between your Church triumphant in Heaven and militant on earth, as members of the same mystical body, where your son Christ Jesus is the head, mercifully grant, that as your blessed saints pray without ceasing for us, we may continually praise and thank you for them, and, in union with their perfect charity, piously celebrate their memories until we all meet before your glorious throne, and with one heart adore the savior of us all; who with you and the Holy Ghost, lives and reigns forever one God, world without end. Amen.

CHAPTER 5: TO ALL ARCHANGELS

"Three Archangels" by Marco d'Oggiono (1490). Courtesy Wikimedia Commons.

Divine Scripture introduces angels seen by all — the angels who appeared to Abraham were seen by him and his whole family; by Lot; the citizens of Sodom and the angel who appeared to Tobias was seen by all present. Since angels don't have bodies naturally united with them, they sometimes assume bodies and appear to be living men even though they really aren't. They assume bodies so their spiritual properties and works can be demonstrated. Their spiritual natures are distinguished from one another in a certain order. The nature of an angel does not prevent him from knowing other angelic natures since both the higher and lower orders of angels share attributes, but differ only according to their various degrees of perfection.

—St. Thomas Aquinas,
Philosopher, Theologian & Doctor of the Church

"*The Three Archangels and Tobias*" *by Francesco Botticini (1470). Courtesy Wikimedia Commons.*

For the Holy Archangels

• *O Lord our God, send your Holy Archangels to our aid and may they, whom always stand before your majesty, present our humble prayers to you for your blessing. Amen.*

Chaplet to the Three Archangels

O God, come to my assistance. Lord, make haste to help me.
 • *Glory be to the Father, and to the Son, and to the Holy Spirit, as it was in the beginning, is now, and ever shall be, world without end. Amen.*

The Apostle's Creed

I believe in God, the Father Almighty, creator of Heaven and earth, and in Jesus Christ, his only son, our Lord: who was conceived by the Holy Spirit, born of the Virgin Mary; suffered under Pontius Pilate, was crucified, died and was buried. He descended into hell; on the third day he rose again from the dead and ascended into Heaven, where he is seated at the right hand of God the Father Almighty.

"St. Michael" by Blasco de Grañén (circa 1445). Courtesy Wikimedia Commons.

From thence he shall come to judge the living and the dead. I believe in the Holy Spirit, the Holy Catholic Church, the communion of saints, the forgiveness of sins, the resurrection of the body, and life everlasting. Amen.

O Holy Spirit, spirit of truth, come into our hearts; shed the brightness of your light upon the nations, that they may please you in unity of faith.

St. Michael, assist me at the hour of death. Bind the evil spirit so it cannot attack or harm my soul.

• *Our Father, who art in Heaven, hallowed be thy name. Thy kingdom come. Thy Will be done, on earth, as it is in Heaven. Give us this day our daily bread and forgive us our trespasses as we forgive those who trespass against us; and lead us not into temptation, but deliver us from evil. Amen.*

• *Hail Mary, full of grace, our Lord is with thee, blessed art thou among women, and blessed is the fruit of thy womb, Jesus. Holy Mary, Mother of God, pray for us sinners, now, and at the hour of our death. Amen*

• *Glory be…*

"St. Gabriel" by Vladimir Borovikovsky (circa 1804). Courtesy Wikimedia Commons.

St. Gabriel, obtain for me a lively faith, a firm hope, a fervent love and a great devotion to the Blessed Sacrament.
* *Our Father...*
* *Hail Mary...*
* *Glory be...*

"Tobias & St. Raphael" by Lorenzo Lippi (1650). Courtesy Wikimedia Commons.

St. Raphael, always lead me on the path of virtue and perfection.
* *Our Father...*
* *Hail Mary...*
* *Glory be...*

"The Archangels Raphael, Michael and Gabriel" by Michele Tosini (1500s).
Courtesy Wikimedia Commons.

To Saints Michael, Gabriel & Raphael

Glorious St. Michael, prince of the heavenly host, protector of the universal Church, defend us against all our visible and invisible enemies, and do not permit that we should ever fall under their cruel tyranny.

St. Gabriel, who, by a just title is called the strength of God, since you were chosen to announce to Mary the mystery wherein the Almighty displayed the force of his arm; cause us to know the treasures contained in the person of the Son of God, and be our protector with his august Mother.

St. Raphael, charitable guide of travelers, you, who by divine power operate miraculous cures, be pleased to guide us in the pilgrimage of this life, and cure the maladies of our souls and bodies. Amen.

CHAPTER 6: ST. MICHAEL, THE ARCHANGEL

"St. Michael" by Claudio Coello (circa 1660). Courtesy Wikimedia Commons.

Michael — which means: "Who is like God?" — is the champion of the primacy of God, of his transcendence and power. Michael fights to reestablish divine justice; he defends the people of God from their enemies and above all from the archenemy, the devil. And St. Michael triumphs because in him it is God who acts. ... Even if the devil is always trying to scratch the face of the Archangel and the face of man, God is stronger; his is the victory and his salvation is offered to every human being. On the journey and in the trials of life we are not alone, we are accompanied and sustained by the Angels of God, who offer, so to speak, their wings to help us overcome the many dangers, to be able to fly above those realities that can make our lives difficult or drag us down.

—Pope Francis

Antiphon to the Archangel Michael

• *Holy Archangel Michael, defend us in battle that we may not be lost in the tremendous judgment. Amen.*

*"Apparition of St. Michael the Archangel and St. Catherine to St. Joan of Arc"
by Hermann Anton Stilke (circa 1800s). Courtesy Wikimedia Commons.*

Prayer to St. Michael
(Approved in 1890 by Pope Leo XIII)

O glorious Archangel St. Michael, prince of the heavenly host, be our defense in the terrible warfare we carry on against principalities and powers, against the rulers of this world of darkness, spirits of evil. Come to the aid of man, whom God created immortal, made in his own image and likeness, and redeemed at a great price from the tyranny of the devil. Fight this day the battle of the Lord, together with the holy angels, as already you fought the leader of the proud angels, Lucifer, and his apostate host, who were powerless to resist you, nor was there place for them any longer in Heaven. That cruel, ancient serpent, who is called the devil or Satan, who seduces the whole world and was cast into the abyss with his angels.

"St. Michael" by Volterrano (1600s). Courtesy Wikimedia Commons.

Behold, this primeval enemy and slayer of men has become bold. Pretending to be an angel of light, he wanders around with all the multitude of wicked spirits, invading the earth to blot out the name of God and of Christ, to seize upon, slay and cast into eternal perdition souls destined for the crown of eternal glory. This wicked dragon pours out the venom of his malice, the spirit of lying, impiety, blasphemy, and the pestilent breath of impurity, and every vice and iniquity.

Arise then, O invincible Prince, bring help against the attacks of the lost spirits to the people of God, and give them victory. They venerate you as their protector and patron; in you the holy Church glories as her defense against the malicious power of hell; to you God entrusted that the souls of men to be established in heavenly beatitude.

Oh, pray to the God of peace to conquer the attacks of Satan so that he may no longer be able to hold men in captivity and harm the Church.

Offer our prayers in the sight of the Most High, so that they may quickly conciliate the mercies of the Lord; and beating down the dragon, the ancient serpent, who is the devil and Satan, again make him captive in the abyss so that he may no longer harm the nations. Amen.

- *Behold the Cross of the Lord; be scattered you hostile powers.*
- **The Lion of the tribe of Judah has conquered, the root of David.**
- *Let your mercies be upon us, O Lord.*
- **As we have hoped in you.**
- *O Lord, hear my prayer.*
- **And let my cry come to you.**

Let Us Pray

O God, the father of our lord Jesus Christ, we call upon your holy name and implore your mercy, that by the intercession of Mary and the glorious Archangel St. Michael, you will help us against Satan and all other unclean spirits, who wander about the world for the injury of the human race and the ruin of souls. Amen.

"St. Michael" by Master of Castelsardo (circa 1480). Courtesy Wikimedia Commons.

Ancient French Prayer to St. Michael

Generous defender of the interests of God, illustrious vanquisher of his enemies, and charitable protector of his children, extend your powerful protection on me, so that I can resist this infernal dragon who you defeated and who has made every effort to devour me. Strengthen me, you illustrious ruler of the angels, and give me your help now and at the hour of my death. This is what we ask through your mercy, O my God, by the merits of Jesus Christ our Savior. Amen.

Novena to St. Michael the Archangel
(Feast Day on September 29)

St. Michael the Archangel, loyal champion of God and his people, I turn to you with confidence and seek your powerful intercession. For the love of God, who made you so glorious in grace and power, and for the love of the Mother of Jesus, the Queen of the Angels, be pleased to hear my prayer.

You know the value on my soul in the eyes of God. May no stain of evil ever disfigure its beauty. Help me to conquer the evil spirit who tempts me. I desire to imitate your loyalty to God and Holy Mother Church and your great love for God and people. Since you are God's messenger for the care of his people, I entrust you with this special request. *(Mention your request).*

St. Michael, since you are, by the will of the Creator, the powerful intercessor of Christians, I have great confidence in your prayers. I earnestly trust that if it is God's holy will, my petition will be granted. Pray for me, St. Michael, and also for those I love. Protect us in all dangers of body and soul. Help us in our daily needs. Through your powerful intercession, may we live a holy life, die a happy death, and reach Heaven where we may praise and love God with you forever. Amen.

In thanksgiving to God for the graces bestowed on St. Michael:

- *Our Father, who art in Heaven, hallowed be thy name. Thy kingdom come. Thy Will be done, on earth, as it is in Heaven. Give us this day our daily bread and forgive us our trespasses as we forgive those who trespass against us; and lead us not into temptation, but deliver us from evil. Amen.*

- *Hail Mary, full of grace, our Lord is with thee, blessed art thou among women, and blessed is the fruit of thy womb, Jesus. Holy Mary, Mother of God, pray for us sinners, now, and at the hour of our death. Amen.*

- *Glory be to the Father and to the Son and to the Holy Spirit. As it was in the beginning is now, and ever shall be, world without end. Amen.*

"St. Michael Weighing Souls" by Juan de la Abadía, 'The Elder' (1480-1495). Courtesy Wikimedia Commons.

For Assistance at the Hour of Death

Glorious Archangel St. Michael, by your protection, enable my soul to be enriched by grace and be worthy to be presented by you to Jesus Christ, my Judge, at the hour of my death. As you conquered Satan and expelled him from Heaven, conquer him again and drive him far away from me at the hour of my death. O Mary, Queen of Heaven, obtain for me the help of St. Michael at the hour of my death! Amen.

For Help Against Spiritual Enemies

Glorious St. Michael, prince of the heavenly hosts, you are always ready to assist the people of God. You fought with the dragon, the old serpent, and cast him out of Heaven, and you now valiantly defend the Church of God so the gates of Hell may never prevail against her. I earnestly ask you to help me also in the painful and dangerous conflict I must sustain against the same formidable foe.

"Archangel Michael" by Riccardo Quartararo (1506). Courtesy Wikimedia Commons.

Be with me, O mighty Prince, so I may courageously fight and wholly vanquish that proud spirit, whom you, by the Divine power, have overthrown, and whom our powerful King, Jesus Christ, in our nature, completely overcame. Then, triumphing over the enemy of my salvation, I may, with you and the holy Angels, praise the mercy of God who grants repentance and forgiveness to mankind. Amen.

Consecration to St. Michael

St. Michael the Archangel, invincible Prince of the Angelic hosts and glorious protector of the universal Church, I greet you and praise you for that splendor with which God has adorned you so richly. I thank God for the great graces he has bestowed on you, especially the grace to remain faithful when Lucifer and his followers rebelled, and to battle victoriously for the honor of God and the Divinity of the Son of Man.

St. Michael, I consecrate to you my soul and body. I choose you as my patron and protector and entrust the salvation of my soul to your care.

Be the guardian of my obligation as a child of God and of the Catholic Church as again I renounce Satan, his works and pomps.

Assist me by your powerful intercession in the fulfillment of these sacred promises, so that by imitating your courage and loyalty to God, and trusting in your kind help and protection, I may be victorious over the enemies of my soul and be united with God in Heaven forever. Amen.

Angelic Crown in Honor of St. Michael the Archangel

O God come to my assistance. Lord make haste to help me.
* *Glory be to the Father and to the Son and to the Holy Spirit. As it was in the beginning is now, and ever shall be, world without end. Amen.*

1. By the intercession of St. Michael and the celestial choir of Seraphim, may the Lord make us worthy to glow with the fire of perfect charity. Amen.
* *Our Father...*
* *Three Hail Marys...*

2. By the intercession of St. Michael and the celestial choir of Cherubim, may the Lord grant us the grace to leave the ways of sin and follow in the paths of Christian perfection. Amen.
* *Our Father...*
* *Three Hail Marys...*

3. By the intercession of St. Michael and the celestial choir of Thrones, may the Lord infuse into our hearts a true and sincere spirit of humility. Amen.

"St. Michael & the Dragon" by Raphael (1483-1520). Courtesy Wikimedia Commons.

- *Our Father...*
- *Three Hail Marys...*

4. By the intercession of St. Michael and the celestial choir of Dominations, may the Lord give us grace to govern our senses and overcome any unruly passions. Amen.

- *Our Father...*
- *Three Hail Marys...*

5. By the intercession of St. Michael and the celestial choir of Virtues, may the Lord preserve us from evil and falling into temptation. Amen.

- *Our Father...*
- *Three Hail Marys...*

6. By the intercession of St. Michael and the celestial choir of Powers, may the Lord protect our souls against the snares and temptations of the devil. Amen.

- *Our Father...*
- *Three Hail Marys...*

7. By the intercession of St. Michael and the celestial choir of Principalities, may God fill our souls with a true spirit of obedience. Amen.
- *Our Father...*
- *Three Hail Marys...*

8. By the intercession of St. Michael and the celestial choir of Archangels, may the Lord give us perseverance in faith and all good works so we may attain the glory of Heaven. Amen.
- *Our Father...*
- *Three Hail Marys...*

9. By the intercession of St. Michael and the celestial choir of Angels, may the Lord grant us to be protected by them in this mortal life and conducted safely to Heaven. Amen.
- *Our Father...*
- *Three Hail Marys...*

*[Say one **Our Father** in honor of each angel below]*

St. Michael…
- *Our Father...*

St. Gabriel…
- *Our Father...*

St. Raphael…
- *Our Father...*

Your Guardian Angel…

- *Our Father...*

O glorious prince St. Michael, chief and commander of the heavenly hosts, guardian of souls, vanquisher of rebel spirits, you who shine with excellence and superhuman virtue deliver us from all evil, who turn to you with confidence and enable us by your gracious protection to serve God more and more faithfully every day. Pray for us, O glorious St. Michael, prince of the Church of Jesus Christ, that we may be made worthy of His promises.

"St. Michael the Archangel" by Juan de Espinal (1780). Courtesy Wikimedia Commons.

Almighty and Everlasting God, who, by a prodigy of goodness and a merciful desire for the salvation of all men, has appointed the most glorious Archangel St. Michael prince of your Church, make us worthy, we ask you, to be delivered from all our enemies, that none of them may harass us at the hour of death, but that we may be conducted by him into your presence. This we ask through the merits of Jesus Christ Our Lord. Amen.

Prayer to St. Michael

St. Michael the Archangel, defend us in battle. Be our protection against the wickedness and snares of the devil. May God rebuke him, we humbly pray; and may you, O prince of the heavenly host, by the power of God, thrust into hell Satan and the other evil spirits who prowl about the world seeking the ruin of souls. Amen.

"St. Michael" by Colijn de Coter (1493-1506). Courtesy Wikimedia Commons.

Short Prayer to St. Michael

Glorious prince of the heavenly hosts and victor over rebellious spirits, be mindful of me who am so weak and sinful and yet so prone to pride and ambition. Lend me, I pray, your powerful aid in every temptation and difficulty, and above all do not forsake me in my last struggle with the powers of evil. Amen.

Prayer to St. Michael for the Church

O glorious prince of the heavenly host, St. Michael, the Archangel, defend us in the warfare we are waging against the principalities and powers, against the rulers of this world of darkness, against the evil spirits. Come to the assistance of men, whom Almighty God created immortal, making them in his own image and likeness and redeeming them at a great price from the tyranny of Satan.

"The Archangel Michael Appearing at Monte Gargano" by Cesare Nebbia (circa 1536-1614). Courtesy Wikimedia Commons.

Fight this day the battle of the Lord with your legions of holy angels, just like when of old you fought against Lucifer, the leader of the proud spirits and all his rebel angels, who were powerless to stand against you.

Neither was their place found anymore in Heaven. And that apostate angel, transformed into an angel of darkness, who still creeps about the earth to encompass our ruin, was cast headlong into the abyss together with his followers.

But, behold, that first enemy of mankind, and a murderer from the beginning, has regained his confidence. Masquerading as an angel of light, he goes about with the whole multitude of the wicked spirits to invade the earth and blot out the name of God and of his Christ, to plunder, to slay, and to consign to eternal damnation the souls that have been destined for a crown of everlasting life. This wicked serpent, like an unclean torrent, pours into men of depraved minds and corrupt hearts the poison of his malice, the spirit of lying, impiety, and blasphemy, and the deadly breath of impurity and every form of vice and iniquity. These crafty enemies of mankind have filled to overflowing with gall and wormwood the Church, which is the Bride of the Lamb without spot. They have laid profane hands upon her most sacred treasures.

Make haste, therefore, O invincible Prince, to help the people of God against the inroads of the lost spirits and grant us the victory. Amen.

Another Prayer to St. Michael for the Church and its Members

O glorious St. Michael, guardian and defender of the Church of Jesus Christ, come to the assistance of this Church, against which the powers of hell are unchained, guard with special care her august head the Pope, and obtain that for him and for us the hour of triumph may speedily arrive. O glorious Archangel St. Michael, watch over us during life, defend us against the assaults of the demon, assist us especially at the hour of death; obtain for us a favorable judgment, and the happiness of beholding God face to face for endless ages. Amen.

Litany after Mass in Honor of St. Michael

Lord, have mercy on us.
Christ, have mercy on us.
Lord, have mercy on us.
Christ, hear us.
Christ, graciously hear us.
God the Father of Heaven, *have mercy on us.*
God the Son, Redeemer of the world, *have mercy on us.*
God the Holy Ghost, *have mercy on us.*
Holy Trinity, one God, *have mercy on us.*
Holy Mary, Queen of the Angels, *pray for us.*

"St. Michael the Archangel Delivers Souls from Purgatory" by Jacopo Vignali (circa 1600s). Courtesy Wikimedia Commons.

St. Michael, the Archangel, *pray for us.*

Most glorious attendant of the Triune Divinity, *pray for us.*

Standing at the right of the altar of Incense, *pray for us.*

Ambassador of Paradise, *pray for us.*

Glorious prince of the heavenly armies, *pray for us.*

Leader of the angelic hosts, *pray for us.*

The standard-bearer of God's armies, *pray for us.*

Defender of divine glory, *pray for us.*

First defender of the Kingship of Christ, *pray for us.*

Strength of God, *pray for us.*

Invincible prince and warrior, *pray for us.*

Angel of Peace, *pray for us.*

Guide of Christ, *pray for us.*

Guardian of the Catholic faith, *pray for us.*

Champion of God's people, *pray for us.*

Guardian Angel of the Eucharist, *pray for us.*
Defender of the Church, *pray for us.*
Protector of the sovereign pontiff, *pray for us.*
Angel of Catholic action, *pray for us.*
Powerful intercessor of Christians, *pray for us.*
Bravest defender of those who hope in God, *pray for us.*
Guardian of our souls and bodies, *pray for us.*
Healer of the sick, *pray for us.*
Help of those in their agony, *pray for us.*
Consoler of the souls in Purgatory, *pray for us.*
God's messenger for the souls of the just, *pray for us.*
Terror of the evil spirits, *pray for us.*
Victorious in battle against evil, *pray for us.*
Guardian and Patron of the universal Church, *pray for us.*
Lamb of God, who takes away the sins of the world, *spare us, O Lord.*

Lamb of God, who takes away the sins of the world, *graciously hear us, O Lord.*

Lamb of God, Who takes away the sins of the world, *have mercy on us.*

- *Pray for us, O glorious St. Michael,*
- *That we may be made worthy of the promises of Christ.*

Let Us Pray

Relying, O Lord, upon the intercession of your blessed Archangel Michael, we humbly beg of you, that the Sacrament of the Eucharist we have received may make our souls holy and pleasing to you. Through Christ our Lord. Amen.

Litany to St. Michael

Lord, have mercy on us.
Christ, have mercy on us.
Lord, have mercy on us.

"St. Michael" by Luca Giordano (1663). Courtesy Wikimedia Commons.

Christ, hear us.

Christ, graciously hear us.

God the Father of Heaven, *have mercy on us.*

God the Son, Redeemer of the world, *have mercy on us.*

God the Holy Spirit, *have mercy on us.*

Holy Trinity, one God, *have mercy on us.*

Holy Mary, Queen of Angels, *pray for us.*

St. Michael, *pray for us.*

St. Michael, filled with the wisdom of God, *pray for us.*

St. Michael, perfect adorer of the Incarnate Word, *pray for us.*

St. Michael, crowned with honor and glory, *pray for us.*

St. Michael, most powerful Prince of the armies of the Lord, *pray for us.*

St. Michael, standard-bearer of the most Holy Trinity, *pray for us.*

St. Michael, guardian of Paradise, *pray for us.*

St. Michael, guide and comforter of the people of Israel, *pray for us.*

St. Michael, splendor and fortress of the Church Militant, *pray for us.*

St. Michael, honor and joy of the Church Triumphant, *pray for us.*

St. Michael, light of Angels, *pray for us.*

St. Michael, bulwark of orthodox believers, *pray for us.*

St. Michael, strength of those who fight under the standard of the Cross, *pray for us.*

St. Michael, light and confidence of souls at the hour of death, *pray for us.*

St. Michael, our most sure aid, *pray for us.*

St. Michael, our help in all adversities, *pray for us.*

St. Michael, herald of the everlasting sentence, *pray for us.*

St. Michael, consoler of souls detained in the flames of Purgatory, *pray for us.*

St. Michael, whom the Lord has charged to receive souls after death, *pray for us.*

St. Michael, our prince, *pray for us.*

St. Michael, our advocate, *pray for us.*

Lamb of God, who takes away the sins of the world, *spare us O Lord.*

Lamb of God, who takes away the sins of the world, *graciously hear us O Lord.*

Lamb of God, who takes away the sins of the world, *have mercy on us.*

Christ, hear us. *Christ, graciously hear us.*

• *Pray for us, O glorious St. Michael, Prince of the Church of Jesus Christ.*

• *That we may be made worthy of his promises.*

Let Us Pray

Sanctify us, we ask you, O Lord Jesus, with your holy blessing, and grant us by the intercession of St. Michael that wisdom which teaches us to lay up treasures in Heaven by exchanging goods of this world for those of eternity, you who lives and reigns world without end. Amen

"St. Michael the Archangel" by Workshop of Garcia Fernandes (1520). Courtesy Wikimedia Commons.

Entrustment Prayer to St. Michael
(Byzantine Catholic prayer)

O great and holy Michael, Archangel of God, standing at the head of the angels before the everlasting Trinity, O advocate and preserver of mankind who, with your hosts, has broken in Heaven the head of the daystar, Satan, the exceedingly proud one, and who always puts to shame his evil and cunning servants on earth, we run to you with faith and pray to you with love: be an unbreakable shield and firm bastion for the Holy Church and for our nation, protecting them with your lightning sword.

Be for us a guardian angel, a wise counselor and helper of our land, bringing to it from the throne of the eternal ruling king and lord our God enlightenment and strength, joy, peace and comfort. Be for us the chief captain and fellow-fighter of our honorable country, crowning it with glory and victory over unjust adversaries, that all who oppose us may know that God and his holy angels stand ready to defend us. Be the physician and healer of those wounded. Be the pillar and defender of those children of the Church of God that are in captivity. And forsake not, O Archangel of God, with your help and protection, those of us who today glorify your holy name. For, behold, though we are great sinners, yet we desire not to perish in our iniquities but to turn to the Lord and be made by him to live for good works.

Illuminate our minds with the light of the countenance of God that shines without ceasing, that we may understand that the will of God concerning us is good and perfect and knows all that is right for us to do, and even that which is right to omit and overlook.

Strengthen by the grace of the Lord our weak and feeble purpose, that made firm in the commandments of the Lord we may cease to wallow in earthly thoughts drawn by the lusts of the flesh as senseless children through the perishable beauties of the world. Above all these things, ask from on high for us the true spirit of repentance, true sorrow and contrition for our sins before God, that we may spend the remaining number of our days in this temporal life, not in satisfying our feelings and in the bondage to our passions, but in blotting out the evil we have done by tears of faith and heartfelt sorrow, by works of charity, chastity, and holy acts of loving mercy.

When the hour of our end and of our liberation from the earthly bonds of our own bodies draws near, O Archangel of God, leave us not without defense against the earthly spirits of evil who try to hinder the entry of man into the heavenly places. Preserved by you, may we, without hindrance, reach those all-glorious dwelling places of paradise where there is neither sorrow nor sighing but only life without end.

May we be made worthy to behold the face of our all-gracious lord and master, and falling at his feet may we cry out in joy and tender feeling:

"The Archangel Michael" by Pere Garcia de Benavarre (circa 1470).
Courtesy Wikimedia Commons.

Glory to you, our most tender, dear redeemer, who, because of your great love for us, your unworthy servants and handmaidens, sent your angels in the service of our salvation!

For all the powers of Heaven praise you, and we give glory, honor and thanksgiving to you, Father, Son and Holy Spirit, now and ever and forever. Amen.

Prayer to St. Michael the Archangel for the Dying

(from the 1800s)

Hail, most glorious St. Michael, hail most merciful leader of the heavenly host! Hail, honor and glory of the angelic hierarchy!

O most illustrious prince, O sublime hero, ornament of Paradise, brilliant jewel of the celestial palace; full of wisdom, perfect in beauty, you are the impress of the divine likeness; gold and precious stones increase your splendor; you walk in the fullness of joy through Paradise; you proceed to the mount of God, through the midst of shining fires; you have been appointed by God, the prince of souls, you raise them up, and bring them into the dwelling of eternal joy.

I venture, blessed prince, to remind you of all the graces which the infinite bounty of God has bestowed upon you above all orders of Angels; and I pray that you by the mutual love of the three Divine Persons, will receive my soul at my last hour, and gain favor for me from the Divine Judge, by the power of your intercession.

Grant the same protection to all the dying, for whom I now intercede, and obtain for them the grace of a holy death. Amen.

CHAPTER 7: ST. RAPHAEL, THE ARCHANGEL

"St. Raphael the Archangel Helping St. John of God" by Bartolomé Esteban Murillo (1672). Courtesy Wikimedia Commons.

Jesus Christ is the center of the angelic world. They are his angels who belong to him because they were created through and for him. They are messengers of his saving plan. Angels have been present since creation and throughout the history of salvation, announcing this salvation and serving the accomplishment of the divine plan. From the Incarnation to the Ascension, the life of the Word Incarnate is surrounded by the adoration and service of angels. They protect Jesus in his infancy, serve him in the desert, strengthen him in his agony in the garden. They evangelize by proclaiming the Good News of Christ's Incarnation and Resurrection. They will be present at Christ's return, which they will announce, to serve at his judgment. The whole life of the Church benefits from the mysterious and powerful help of angels. And the Church invokes their assistance and celebrates the memory of certain angels, especially St. Michael, St. Gabriel, St. Raphael, and the guardian angels.

—*The Vatican*

"The Archangel Raphael and Tobias with Saints James and Nicholas" by Cima da Conegliano (1460-1518). Courtesy Wikimedia Commons.

Prayer for St. Raphael's Spiritual Help

O God who in your ineffable goodness has rendered blessed Raphael the conductor of your faithful in their journeys, we humbly implore you that we may be conducted by him in the way of salvation, and experience his help in the maladies of our souls. Through Jesus Christ our Lord. Amen.

For the Assistance of St. Raphael

O most glorious Prince, Raphael the Archangel, remember us here and everywhere. Pray always to the Son of God for us, *Alleluia, Alleluia.*

- *An Angel stood near the altar of the temple.*
- *Holding a golden censer in his hand.*

O God, who gave blessed Raphael the Archangel to Tobias your servant as a companion for his journey, grant that we, who are also your servants, may also be safeguarded by his watchfulness and fortified by his help. Through our Lord Jesus Christ. Amen.

Holy Communion Prayer to St. Raphael

Grant, O Lord God, to send to our assistance St. Raphael the Archangel, and may he, who, we believe, evermore stands before the throne of your majesty, offer to you our humble petitions to be blessed by you. Through Christ our Lord. Amen.

"Curing the Blindness of Tobias's Father" by Antonio de Pereda (1652). Courtesy Wikimedia Commons.

Prayer to St. Raphael, the Archangel

Glorious archangel, St. Raphael, great prince of the heavenly court, illustrious by your gifts of wisdom and grace, guide of travelers by air, land and sea, consoler of the unfortunate and refuge of sinners, I ask you to help me in all my needs and in all the trials of this life as you did once assist the young Tobias in his journeying.

And since you are the "physician of God," I humbly ask you to heal my soul of its many infirmities and my body of the ills that afflict it, if this favor is for my greater good. I ask, especially, for angelic purity, that I may be made fit to be the living temple of the Holy Ghost. Amen.

"*The Archangel Raphael" by unknown (1700s). Courtesy Wikimedia Commons.*

Prayer to St. Raphael

O heavenly physician and faithful companion St. Raphael, who restored sight to the elder Tobias, and guided the younger in his long journey and preserved him in safety, by the physician of my soul and body, disperse the dark clouds of ignorance, defend me from the dangers of my earthly pilgrimage, and lead me to that heavenly country where, with you, I may gaze forever on the face of God. Amen.

Prayer of the Church in Honor of St. Raphael Archangel

O Lord God, send to our assistance St. Raphael the Archangel, and may he, who, we believe, evermore stands before the throne of your Majesty, offer to you our humble petitions to be blessed by you. Through Christ our Lord. Amen.

"The Archangel Raphael Refusing Tobias's Gift" by Giovanni Biliverti (1612). Courtesy Wikimedia Commons.

Prayer to St. Raphael, Angel of Happy Meetings

O Raphael, lead us towards those we are waiting for, those who are waiting for us! Raphael, angel of happy meetings, lead us by the hand towards those we are looking for! May all our movements, all their movements, be guided by your light and transfigured by your joy.

Angel guide of Tobias, lay the request we now address to you at the feet of Him on whose unveiled face you are privileged to gaze. Lonely and tired, crushed by the separations and sorrows of earth, we feel the need to call you and ask for the protection of your wings.

Remember the weak, you who are strong, you whose home lies beyond the region of thunder, in a land that is always peaceful, always serene, and bright with the resplendent glory of God. Amen.

"The Archangel and Tobias" by unknown (1600s). Courtesy Wikimedia Commons.

Prayers to St. Raphael and the Holy Angels for Travelers

May the almighty and merciful Lord direct us on our journey; may he make it prosper and maintain us in peace. May the Archangel Raphael accompany us along the way and may we return to our homes in peace, joy, and health.

- *Lord, have mercy on us!*
- *Jesus Christ, have mercy on us!*
- *Lord, have mercy on us!*

O God, who enabled the children of Israel to traverse the Red Sea dry; you who pointed out by a star to the Magi the road that led them to you; grant us we ask you, a prosperous journey and propitious weather; so that, under the guidance of your holy angels we may safely reach that journey's end, and later the haven of eternal salvation.

Hear, O Lord, the prayers of your servants. Bless their travels. You who are everywhere present, shower everywhere upon them the effects of your mercy; so that, insured by your protection against all dangers, they may return to offer you their thanksgiving. Through Christ our Lord. Amen.

"Marriage bed of Tobias & Sarah" by Jan Steen (1660). Courtesy Wikimedia Commons.

Novena to St. Raphael the Archangel
(Feast Day on September 29)

Holy Archangel Raphael, standing so close to the throne of God and offering him our prayers, I venerate you as God's special friend and messenger. I choose you as my patron and wish to love and obey you as young Tobias did. I consecrate to you my body and soul, all my work, and my whole life. I want you to be my guide and Counselor in all the dangerous and difficult problems and decisions of my life.

Remember dearest St. Raphael, that the grace of God preserved you with the good Angels in Heaven when the proud ones were cast into hell. I entreat you, therefore, to help me in my struggle against the world, the spirit of impurity, and the devil.

Defend me from all dangers and every occasion of sin. Direct me always in the way of peace, safety, and salvation. Offer my prayers to God as you offered those of Tobias, so that through your intercession I may obtain the graces necessary for the salvation of my soul. I ask you to pray to God to grant me this favor if it be his holy will. *(Mention your request.)*

Raphael, help me to love and serve my God faithfully, to die in his grace, and finally join you in seeing and praising God forever in Heaven. Amen.

Novena in Honor of
St. Raphael the Archangel

- *O God, come to my assistance;*
- *O Lord, make haste to help me.*
- *Glory be to the Father, and to the Son, and to the Holy Spirit, as it was in the beginning, is now, and ever shall be, world without end. Amen.*

O Christ, Splendor of the Father, life and strength of the heart, in the presence of the Angels we celebrate you by our prayers and hymns, uniting our voices with their melodious concerts. We praise with reverence all the celestial Princes, but especially the Archangel St. Raphael, the faithful companion by whose power the Devil was enchained.

O Christ, King full of goodness, by this guardian remove far from us all the wickedness of the enemy; purify our hearts and our bodies, and by your sole clemency, introduce us into Paradise. In harmonious concerts let us give thanks to the Father, glory to Jesus Christ and to the Comforter, God three in One, living before all ages. Amen.

- *Hail Mary, full of grace, our Lord is with thee, blessed art thou among women, and blessed is the fruit of thy womb, Jesus. Holy Mary, Mother of God, pray for us sinners, now, and at the hour of our death. Amen*
- *Pray for us, St. Raphael,*
- *That we may be made worthy of the promises of Christ.*

Let Us Pray

O God, who gave to your servant Tobias, on his journey, the blessed Raphael the Archangel for a companion; grant that we who are also your servants, may likewise be safeguarded by his watchfulness, and be made strong by his help. May he who stands before your majesty offer up our prayers to be blessed by you; through Jesus Christ, Our Lord. Amen.

"St. Raphael Leaves Tobias & his family" by Jan Victors (1649). Courtesy Wikimedia Commons.

Prayer to St. Raphael for Emigrants

St. Raphael the Archangel, you were a faithful companion to the young man, Tobias, on his long journey from Syria to Media. You rescued him from many dangers, especially from death in the river Tigris. We ask you with all our hearts to be a safe guide and an angel of consolation to our dear ones on their long journey they must take to travel to foreign lands. Keep them far from all dangers of body and soul, and grant they come safely to their destination.

• *Glory be to the Father, and to the Son, and to the Holy Spirit, as it was in the beginning, is now, and ever shall be, world without end. Amen*

St. Raphael the Archangel, arriving in Media you bestowed on the young Tobias extraordinary favors, yourself going to the city of Rages to receive money from Gabelus, and helping Tobias find a worthy spouse in Sara, when she was delivered from the slavery of the demon, and enriching him with good fortune. Look, we humbly ask you, on our dear ones who find themselves in foreign lands and also extend to them your heavenly protection, prospering their labors to benefit our beloved families and saving them from the many snares that will be laid for their souls so they may be able to preserve the precious gift of faith and conform their lives to its teaching.

- *Glory be...*

"Tobias & the Angel" by Girolamo Savoldo (circa 1525). Courtesy Wikimedia Commons.

St. Raphael the Archangel, faithful to your mission you brought back safely to Syria the young Tobias, enriching his house with blessings and graces, even restoring the gift of sight to his blind father; fulfill your task on behalf of our dear emigrants. Bring them back in your own good time, safe and sound, to our dear families, and grant that their return may be a source of consolation and prosperity with every blessing. We too, like the family of Tobias, will thank you for all your tender care and join you in praising, blessing and thanking God, the giver of every good and perfect gift. Amen.

- *Glory be...*
- **Pray for us, St. Raphael the Archangel, that we may be made worthy of the promises of Christ.**

Let Us Pray

O God, who gave your blessed Archangel Raphael to your servant Tobias to be his fellow traveler; grant to us that he may always keep us and shield us, help us and defend us. Through Christ our Lord. Amen.

"Tobias & the Angel" by Eduardo Rosales (circa 1860). Courtesy Wikimedia Commons.

Litany of St. Raphael

Lord, have mercy on us.
Christ have mercy on us.
Lord, have mercy on us.
Christ hear us.
Christ, graciously hear us.
God the Father of Heaven, *have mercy on us.*
God the Son, Redeemer of the world, *have mercy on us.*
God the Holy Spirit, *have mercy on us.*
Holy Trinity, One God, *have mercy on us.*
Holy Mary, Queen of Angels, *pray for us.*
St. Raphael, *pray for us.*
St. Raphael, filled with the mercy of God, *pray for us.*
St. Raphael, perfect adorer of the Divine Word, *pray for us.*
St. Raphael, terror of demons, *pray for us.*
St. Raphael, exterminator of vices, *pray for us.*
St. Raphael, health of the sick, *pray for us.*
St. Raphael, our refuge in all our trials, *pray for us.*
St. Raphael, guide of travelers, *pray for us.*

St. Raphael, consoler of prisoners, *pray for us.*

St. Raphael, joy of the sorrowful, *pray for us.*

St. Raphael, filled with zeal for the salvation of souls, *pray for us.*

St. Raphael, whose name means "God heals," *pray for us.*

St. Raphael, lover of chastity, *pray for us.*

St. Raphael, scourge of demons, *pray for us.*

St. Raphael, in pestilence, famine and war, *pray for us.*

St. Raphael, angel of peace and prosperity, *pray for us.*

St. Raphael, endowed with the grace of healing, *pray for us.*

St. Raphael, sure guide in the paths of virtue and sanctification, *pray for us.*

St. Raphael, help of all those who implore your assistance, *pray for us.*

St. Raphael, who was the guide and consolation of Tobias on his journey, *pray for us.*

St. Raphael, whom the Scriptures praises as: *"Raphael, the holy Angel of the Lord, was sent to cure," pray for us.*

St. Raphael, our advocate, *pray for us.*

Lamb of God, who takes away the sins of the world, *spare us, O Lord.*

Lamb of God, who takes away the sins of the world, *graciously hear us, O Lord.*

Lamb of God, who takes away the sins of the world, *have mercy on us.*

Christ, hear us. *Christ, graciously hear us.*

Pray for us, St. Raphael, to the Lord Our God, that we may be made worthy of the promises of Christ.

Let Us Pray

Lord, Jesus Christ, by the prayer of the Archangel Raphael, grant us the grace to avoid all sin and to persevere in every good work until we reach our Heavenly destination, you who lives and reigns world without end. Amen.

Chapter 8: St. Gabriel, the Archangel

"The Annunciation" by Orazio Gentileschi (circa 1623). Courtesy Wikimedia Commons.

The Angel Gabriel proclaimed: "The Holy Spirit will come upon you, and the power of the Most High will overshadow you; therefore the child to be born will be called holy, the Son of God". We repeat these words when we recite the Creed: "and by the Holy Spirit was incarnate of the Virgin Mary." Sometimes, on our journey and in our life of faith, we can sense our poverty, our inadequacy in the face of the witness we must offer to the world. However God chose, precisely, a humble woman, in an unknown village, in one of the most distant provinces of the great Roman Empire.

We must always trust in God, even in the face of the most grueling difficulties, renewing our faith in his presence and action in our history, just as in Mary's. Nothing is impossible to God! With him our existence always journeys on safe ground and is open to a future of firm hope. This is an announcement that rings out ever new and brings hope and joy to our hearts because, every time, it gives us the certainty that even though we often feel weak, poor and incapable in the face of difficulties and evil in the world, God's power is always active and works miracles through weakness itself. His grace is our strength.

—Pope Benedict XVI

"Angel of the Annunciation" by Guido Reni (circa 1600). Courtesy Wikimedia Commons.

Prayer for St. Gabriel's Assistance

O God who in preference to any other of your angels, chose blessed Gabriel to announce the mystery of your incarnation, grant to us, who venerate him on earth, the help of his patronage in Heaven. Amen.

"St. Gabriel" by Filippo Lippi (circa 1450). Courtesy Wikimedia Commons.

Short Prayer to the Archangel Gabriel

Blessed Archangel Gabriel, we ask you to intercede for us at the throne of divine mercy in our present necessities that, as you announced to Mary the mystery of the incarnation, so through your prayers and patronage in heaven we may sing the praise of God forever in the land of the living. Amen.

"The Annunciation" by Heinrich Johann Sinkel (1862). Courtesy Wikimedia Commons.

Prayer to the St. Gabriel the Archangel

O loving messenger of the Incarnation, descend upon all those for whom I wish peace and happiness. Spread your wings over the cradles of the newborn babies, O you who did announce the coming of the infant Jesus.

Give to young people a lily petal from the virginal scepter in your hand. Cause the Ave Maria to re-echo in all hearts that they may find grace and joy through Mary. Finally, recall the sublime words spoken on the day of the Annunciation—"Nothing is impossible with God," and repeat them in hours of trial—to all I love—that their confidence in Our Lord may be reanimated when all human help fails. Amen.

Archangel Gabriel, Troparion

Gabriel, commander of the heavenly hosts, we ask you by your prayers to encompass us beneath the wings of your glory and faithfully preserve us who cry to you: *"Deliver us from all harm, for you are the Commander of the powers on high!"* Amen.

"The Vision of Daniel with St. Gabriel" by Willem Drost (1650). Courtesy Wikimedia Commons.

Prayer to St. Gabriel

O Gabriel, might of God, who did announce to the Virgin Mary the incarnation of the only Son of God, and in the garden did console and strengthen Christ oppressed with fear and sorrow; I praise you, O chosen spirit, and humbly pray you to be my advocate with Jesus Christ my Savior, and with Mary, his blessed Virgin Mother; in all my trials do assist me, lest overcome by temptation I offend my God and Sovereign Good. Amen.

Novena to St. Gabriel the Archangel
(Feast Day on September 29)

St. Gabriel the Archangel, I venerate you as the "Angel of the Incarnation," because God especially appointed you to bear the messages concerning the God-Man to Daniel, Zechariah, and the Blessed Virgin Mary. Give me a tender and devoted mother in Mary. Amen.

"The Angel Announcing to Zechariah the Forthcoming Nativity of St. John the Baptist" by Simão Rodrigues (circa 1597-1621).

I venerate you also as the "strength from God," because you are the giver of God's strength, consoler and comforter chosen to strengthen God's faithful and to teach them important truths. I ask for the grace of a special power of the will to strive for holiness of life. Steady my resolutions, renew my courage, comfort and console me in the problems, trials, and sufferings of daily living, as you consoled our Savior in his agony and Mary in her sorrows and Joseph in his trials. I put my confidence in you.

St. Gabriel, I ask you especially for this favor. *(Mention your request.)* Through your earnest love for the son of God-made-man and for his blessed Mother, I beg of you, intercede for me that my request may be granted, if it be God's holy Will. Pray for us, St. Gabriel the Archangel. That we may be made worthy of the promises of Christ.

Let Us Pray

Almighty and ever-living God, since you chose the Archangel Gabriel from among all the Angels to announce the mystery of your Son's Incarnation, mercifully grant that we who honor him on earth may feel the benefit of his patronage in Heaven. You who live and reign forever. Amen.

"The Annunciation" by Philippe de Champaigne (circa 1645). Courtesy Wikimedia Commons.

Litany of St. Gabriel

Lord, have mercy on us.

Christ, have mercy on us.

Lord, have mercy on us.

Christ, hear us.

Christ, graciously hear us.

God the Father of Heaven, *have mercy on us.*

God the Son, Redeemer of the world, *have mercy on us.*

God the Holy Spirit, *have mercy on us.*

Holy Trinity, One God, *have mercy on us.*

Holy Mary, Queen of Angels, *pray for us.*

St. Gabriel, glorious Archangel, *pray for us.*

St. Gabriel, strength of God, *pray for us.*

St. Gabriel, who stands before the throne of God, *pray for us.*

St. Gabriel, model of prayer, *pray for us.*

St. Gabriel, herald of the Incarnation, *pray for us.*

St. Gabriel, who revealed the glories of Mary, *pray for us.*

St. Gabriel, prince of Heaven, *pray for us.*

St. Gabriel, ambassador of the Most High, *pray for us.*

St. Gabriel, guardian of the Immaculate Virgin, *pray for us.*

St. Gabriel, who foretold the greatness of Jesus, *pray for us.*

St. Gabriel, peace and light of souls, *pray for us.*

St. Gabriel, scourge of unbelievers, *pray for us.*

St. Gabriel, admirable teacher, *pray for us.*

St. Gabriel, strength of the just, *pray for us.*

St. Gabriel, protector of the faithful, *pray for us.*

St. Gabriel, first adorer of the Divine Word, *pray for us.*

St. Gabriel, defender of the faith, *pray for us.*

St. Gabriel, zealous for the honor of Jesus Christ, *pray for us.*

St. Gabriel, whom the Scriptures praise as the Angel sent by God to Mary, the Virgin, *pray for us.*

Lamb of God, who takes away the sins of the world, *spare us, O Lord.*

Lamb of God, who takes away the sins of the world, *graciously hear us, O Lord.*

Lamb of God, who takes away the sins of the world, *have mercy on us.*

Christ, hear us. *Christ, graciously hear us.*

- *Pray for us, blessed Archangel Gabriel,*
- *That we may be made worthy of the promises of Jesus Christ.*

Let Us Pray

O blessed Archangel Gabriel, we ask you, intercede for us at the throne of Divine Mercy in our present necessities, that as you announced to Mary the mystery of the Incarnation, so through your prayers and patronage in Heaven we may obtain the benefits of the same, and sing the praise of God forever in the land of the living. Amen.

CHAPTER 9: REFERENCES

• Chapter 1:"The Life of St. Teresa of Jesus of the Order of Our Lady of Carmel"by St. Teresa of Avila (prior to 1567), http://www.gutenberg.org/dirs/etext05/8trsa10h.htm.

• Chapter 2:"General Audience, Castel Gandolfo,"Pope Benedict XVI (Aug. 22, 2012),http://www.vatican.va/holy_father/benedict_xvi/audiences/2012/documents/hf_ben-xvi_aud_20120822_en.html.

• Chapter 3:"Padre Pio Letters"in The Writings of the Saints from Opus Sanctorum Angelorum, http://www.opusangelorum.org/angels_saints/angels_saints.html.

• Chapter 4:"Fatima Apparition of the Angel,"from Fatima Family Apostolate International (Nov. 25, 2011), http://www.fatimafamily.org/fatima-apparition-of-the-angel/.

• Chapter 5:"Treatise on the Angels"in Summa Theologica, by St. Thomas Aquinas (1265–1274), http://www.gutenberg.org/cache/epub/17611/pg17611.html.

• Chapter 6:"Blessing of the New Statue of St. Michael the Archangel in theVatican Gardens,"in Address of the Holy Father Francis (July 5, 2013).

• Chapter 7:"The Opus Sanctorum Angelorum" (March 2011) http://www.vatican.va/roman_curia/congregations/cfaith/documents/rc_con_cfaith_doc_20110316_nota-opus-angelorum_en.html.

• Chapter 8:"General Audience,"Pope Benedict XVI (Jan. 2, 2013), http://www.vatican.va/holy_father/benedict_xvi/audiences/2013/documents/hf_ben-xvi_aud_20130102_en.html

About the Author: Marie Noël

Marie Noël is an ordinary person living an ordinary life. Her love of Catholicism, interests in history, and quest to deepen her faith have led her to share this collection of prayers. Visit her website, Facebook page, or Twitter for information on her latest prayer collections. She regularly posts historic prayers & images there.

www.booksbynoel.com

Twitter: BooksByNoel

Facebook: http://on.fb.me/YK9XOq

Finis, Gloria in Altissimis Deo

Other Prayer Collections by Marie Noël

Did you enjoy Prayers to the Holy Angels? Here are some other titles that you may be interested in. They are all illustrated with beautiful photos as well as European religious paintings and drawings from the Renaissance. Available in eBook and paperback.

Catholic Prayers of Thanks

This collection of prayers features devotions from the late 1700s through the 1800s. 60+ prayers are prayers of thanks: to God, Jesus Christ, the Holy Spirit, the Trinity, and the Blessed Sacrament; regarding the Church sacraments such as Mass and Confession; for each day and special occasions (your birthday, on becoming a mother, etc.); and favors granted.

Catholic Christmas Prayers

A wonderful treasury of Christmas prayers to help prepare for this special holy season. 20+ Roman Catholic prayers, including Novenas and Litanies, in categories such as: for Advent; to the Christ Child; for Christmas Eve and Christmas Day; and for Epiphany.

Catholic Prayers to the King & Queen of Heaven... with prayers for kings & queens on Earth

This book is the first in a Royal Saint Series, dedicated to the little-known saintly Catholic rulers of former times. Dedicated to Jesus and Mary, it contains rare prayers from as old as the 11th century. Featuring prayers to honor the King and Queen of Heaven, invoke the intercession of royal medieval saints, and also to seek intercession for today's kings and queens.

Catholic Prayers to Saintly Germanic Kings & Queens

This second book in the Royal Saint Series features saints of Germanic origin. Included are 50+ ancient and medieval prayers to these unique Catholic saints. Also included are prayers to Jesus and Mary, prayers for the present-day countries of these saints, and litanies to popular medieval saints. Many of these prayers are from the Middle Ages and have been translated from French, German & Latin. The book features brief historical biographies for each saint and is illustrated with beautiful photos and European religious paintings from the Renaissance.

.

Made in the USA
Columbia, SC
02 July 2022

62633718R00088